SOCIO-ECONOMIC REVIEW 2002

Socio-Economic Review 2002

An Agenda For Fairness

Ensuring
- Economic Development
- Social Equity
- Sustainability

CORI
Justice Commission

ISBN No. 1 872335 57 8

First Published: February 2002

Published by:
CORI Justice Commission
Tabor House
Milltown Park
Dublin 6
Ireland

Tel: 01-269 7799
Fax: 01-269 8887

e-mail: justice@cori.ie

TABLE OF CONTENTS

1.	**INTRODUCTION**	1
2.	**CONTEXT**	4
2.1	Economic Review and Outlook	4
2.2	Social Progress	5
2.3	Poverty	6
2.4	National Action Plan against Poverty and Social Exclusion	21
2.5	National Anti-Poverty Strategy Review 2002	22
2.6	Unemployment	23
2.7	Income Distribution	25
2.8	Social Exclusion	29
2.9	An Agenda for Fairness	32
3.	**AN AGENDA FOR FAIRNESS**	33
	Objectives, Analysis & Policy Proposals	
3.1	Income	33
3.2	Taxation	41
3.3	Work	61
3.4	Public Services	66
3.5	Accommodation	69
3.6	Healthcare	82
3.7	Education	90
3.8	Culture and Cultural Respect	103
3.9	Participation	108
3.10	Promoting Sustainability	113
3.11	Rural Development	123
3.12	Official Development Assistance	128
4.	**VALUES**	132
5.	**CONCLUSION**	137
	REFERENCES	139

1. INTRODUCTION

There is a major paradox at the heart of Irish development. Despite the unprecedented economic growth of the Irish economy in recent years and its accompanying prosperity there has been a marked failure to address adequately the issues of social cohesion and infrastructure deficit that are still problematic throughout the country. While Ireland now has a per capita income well above the EU average its infrastructure and social provision are far below the EU level. At the same time Ireland's tax-take is far below the EU average and this is seen as a virtue to be protected at all costs. This combination of circumstances raises the question: how can Ireland have an EU level of infrastructure and social provision if it is not prepared to pay EU levels of taxation? Or alternatively, is Ireland satisfied to continue with levels of infrastructure and social provision well below the EU average and live with the lower quality of life that accompanies such lower levels of provision?

There have been many positive developments to record in recent years. Economic growth has been at unprecedented levels. Despite the recent slowdown it is still higher than most EU and OECD countries. The numbers employed have grown dramatically. There has been a substantial fall in the numbers unemployed. The rate of long-term unemployment is much lower today than it was a decade ago.

Many argue, however, that in recent years Ireland has had prosperity without fairness. While the wealth of the nation has grown dramatically, the proportion of the population with incomes below the poverty line (set at half average income, adjusted for family size and composition) has also grown. The proportion of households below the same poverty line has also grown. The gap between the better off and the poor has widened dramatically. There is growing social polarisation between these two parts of society. This situation has been exacerbated by most of the recent Budgets which saw those who were already better off gaining most when the available resources were allocated.

There has been a growing debate about the model of society that Irish people wish to see evolve. This has been encapsulated in the rather misleading phrase 'Boston or Berlin' which has been used to contrast the 'European' model with the 'American' model. It could be argued that Ireland has been moving towards the American model of socio-economic development which is characterised by low taxation, more emphasis on the responsibilities of individuals, less social provision and growing inequality.

We now have a situation where the share of GNP going on wages is much lower than it was a decade ago. At the same time the share going on profits is markedly higher. Likewise, the share of GNP going on social welfare payments is markedly lower than it was before the advent of the economic boom. While this in part is a consequence of the decline in the numbers unemployed, it is also a consequence of the failure to use the available resources to raise the standard of living of Ireland's poorest so as to bring them above the relative income poverty line. Despite claims to the contrary from a range of sources the reality is that Ireland's rate of relative income poverty has risen during the boom years and is one of the highest in the EU

A reversal of recent trends in these areas seems more than desirable if Ireland is to have a *fair* distribution of its new resources. A major challenge facing policy makers, the social partnership process, political parties and the political process generally is to address this key issue of the lack of fairness in the distribution of the fruits of economic growth. If these various processes do not give a much higher priority to social spending than has been the case heretofore then the unfairness of the present situation will deepen, the gaps in society will widen even further and we will be left with a deeply divided two-tier society.

Fairness does not emerge spontaneously or automatically. It has to be worked for and developed in concrete policy initiatives rooted in a strategy that acknowledges that fairness is a desired outcome. While there has been much favourable rhetoric in this area concrete initiatives and strategies have been lacking. For the most part the strategies and policies followed to date have taken a minimalist approach focusing on the eradication of *absolute* or *consistent* poverty. Such an approach ignores core issues of equality and distributive justice and will not produce a fair society. This situation must be reversed.

We welcome the substantial commitment contained in the recently published review of the National Anti-Poverty Strategy on raising the lowest social welfare payment to 30% of average industrial income by 2007. We regret, however, that much greater progress towards reaching such a target was not made during the recent years of great economic growth.

Irish society is faced with substantial opportunities, challenges and choices at this time. The future that emerges will result from the decisions taken at this time. An agenda for fairness is required. The details of such an agenda are spelt out in this socio-economic review. In presenting our analysis and proposals we pay special attention to how Ireland is experienced today by those who have not done so well from the economic growth of recent years. All our proposals are presented within responsible fiscal policy parameters.

We do not claim to have all the answers. However, we present our analysis and make our proposals as a contribution to the public debate on what the key priorities in the socio-economic arena should be in the years ahead. All responses are most welcome.

2. CONTEXT

2.1 Economic Review and Outlook

Growth

The Irish economy continues to retain its title as the fastest growing economy within both the EU and the OECD. However, in the context of an international economic slowdown the scale of the economy's success is changing. During 2001 real GDP grew by 4.7 per cent (ESRI, 2001), a figure that is noticeably smaller than the growth rates achieved throughout the past five years. That decline impacted on unemployment which increased for the first time since 1996 to a rate of 4.3 per cent, while employment rose by 76,300. Concurrent with the economic slowdown, the public finances have deteriorated and the current account of the balance of payments records a deficit equalling 0.7 per cent of GNP (ESRI, 2001). Predictions of real GDP growth in 2002 vary noticeably. The ESRI and the IMF predict a rate of 3 per cent while the Department of Finance more optimistically maintains that growth will be 3.9 per cent. The latter's optimism may cause further public finance difficulties if its prediction is proven incorrect. All agree, however, that the international slowdown is short-term and that after 2002 annualised growth rates should return to over 4 per cent.

Inflation

In 2000, high rates of inflation (price increases) were threatening competitiveness and undermining the value of increases secured under *The Programme for Prosperity and Fairness* (PPF). In November 2000, the annual rate of inflation, as measured by the Consumer Price Index (CPI), climbed to 7 per cent. Since then it has reduced to an annual rate of 4.9 per cent. However, Irish inflation remains well above the European average of 2.0%.

The main factors contributing to these price increases are the rising costs of services, higher entertainment prices, rising insurance premiums, higher rents and increases in the price of alcoholic drink, tobacco and food. The decline in inflation results from lower fuel, clothing and mortgage costs (lower interest rates).

Forecasts for 2002 suggest that inflation will further decrease to 3.7 per cent (ESRI, 2001), a figure still substantially higher than the European average. These sustained high rates of inflation continue to undermine the real value of all the increases agreed within the PPF. The pay, tax and social inclusion elements of the programme were negotiated on a forecast that inflation would have an annual average of just over 3 per cent throughout the three-year period of the agreement.

2.2 Social Progress

Increasingly it is recognised that the progress of any society must be broadly measured to include factors other than economic growth rates. Simply, 'people are the real wealth of nations' (UNDP, 2001), and therefore the central aim of society must be to create what the United Nations Human Development Report (2001) describes as 'an environment in which people can develop their full potential and lead productive, creative lives in accord with their needs and interests'. Economic growth is therefore not an end in itself, but rather a means to facilitate the achievement of a more equal and inclusive society.

The United Nations Development Index offers the best available measurement of the quality of life offered in countries across the world. It assesses countries on a range of socio-economic indicators including life expectancy, education, literacy and adjusted real income. It also contains tables of other indicators such as economic growth, health status, poverty, personal distress and information flow. Ireland is placed eighteenth on the 2001 index, an unchanged position since 2000.

Ireland performs well according to the economic indicators, and has the seventh highest GDP per capita. However, the social indicators record a significantly poorer performance. A total of 22.6 per cent of the Irish population are identified as being functionally illiterate, meaning that they are unable to read basic texts or a newspaper. Similarly, the provision of health care in Ireland compares poorly with that of other countries. The proportion of GDP spent on healthcare by the Irish Government is 4.5 per cent. This compares with 7.9 per cent in both Germany and Belgium, 7.3 per cent in France, 7.4 per cent in Norway, 5.8 per cent in the USA and 5.9 per cent in the UK. Throughout Europe, the governments of countries such as Greece, Portugal, Slovenia, Poland and Lithuania all allocate a greater proportion of GDP to health expenditure. The number of doctors per 100,000 of the population provides a further indication of the low level of public healthcare expenditure. Ireland has only 219 doctors per 100,000 of the population, compared with 312 in Portugal, 413 in Norway, 350 in Germany and 395 in Belgium. Across the EU only the UK records a lower figure, with 164 doctors per 100,000.

Consequently, it is of no surprise that the health status of the Irish population compares unfavourably with that of other developed countries. Life expectancy at birth in Ireland is 76.1 years, compared to 80 in Japan and 78 in Norway, France, Italy and Spain.

2.3 Poverty

The extent of poverty in Ireland has been highlighted by the UN Human Development Report (2001). Of seventeen industrialised countries, Ireland is ranked sixteenth on the poverty index. Only the USA has a higher percentage of its population living in poverty. The UK is ranked fifteenth, while Sweden, Norway and the Netherlands are the countries with the lowest levels of poverty. The variables used in this measurement of poverty are the percentages of people likely to die before age 60, people who are functionally illiterate, people with disposable incomes less than 50 per cent of the median, and those unemployed for more than a year. All the major countries of Europe do better than Ireland where poverty is concerned.

In the context of sustained levels of record economic growth, the scale of poverty in Ireland can surprise many. Taken as a whole, the Republic of Ireland has become a much more prosperous place. However, the distribution of that prosperity has been such that the 'Celtic Tiger' dividend has been non-existent for a large number of this country's citizens.

Who are the poor?

How many people are poor? On what basis are they classified as poor? In trying to measure the extent of poverty, the most common approach has been to identify a poverty line (or lines) based on people's incomes. Where that line should be drawn is sometimes a contentious matter, but many European studies (including those carried out by the ESRI in Ireland) now suggest *a line, which is half average income, adjusted for family size and composition.* Alternatives set at 40 per cent and 60 per cent of average income are also used fairly often to clarify and lend robustness to conclusions that could impact on policy.

- In financial terms the ESRI discovered that the income-per-adult equivalent averaged over households in 1998 was €237.73 (£187.23). Consequently, the income poverty lines for a single adult derived from this average were:

    40 per cent line — €95.09 (£74.89) a week
    50 per cent line — €118.86 (£93.61) a week
    60 per cent line — €142.64 (£112.34) a week

- Updating the more generally accepted poverty line (i.e. 50 per cent of average income) to 2002 levels, using actual (CSO, 98–2001) and predicted (Department of Finance, 2002) increases in average industrial earnings, produces a relative income poverty line of €157.71 (£124.21) for a single person. This is €33.91 (£30.65) more than the current level of most social assistance rates.

The most up-to-date data available on poverty in Ireland come from the 1998 Living in Ireland Survey, conducted by the ESRI, and is shown in Table 1.

Table 1: Percentage of households and persons below relative income poverty lines 1994/1997/1998							
	Households			Persons		
	1994	1997	1998	1994	1997	1998
40% line	4.8	6.3	10.5	5.2	6.3	9.1
50% line	18.6	22.4	24.6	17.4	18.1	20.0
60% line	34.1	34.3	33.4	30.4	30.1	28.6

Source: Derived from Layte et al. (2001: 14–15)

- Overall the 40 and 50 per cent lines show a continued increase in the numbers below those lines for the whole period. Only the 60 per cent line shows a minor decrease.
- Using the more generally accepted poverty line (50 per cent) the percentage of *persons* under this line rose from 17.4 per cent in 1994 to 18.1 per cent in 1997, and increased further to 20 per cent in 1998.
- Similarly, *households* experiencing poverty increased, with the equivalent numbers being 18.6 per cent, 22.4 per cent and 24.6 per cent respectively.
- In summary, we can use the 50 per cent line to conclude that one in four households and one in five persons live in poverty.

The depth of poverty experienced by people and households has declined between 1994 and 1998. Even though people remain relatively poor, they do have more money in their pockets. Therefore, those below relative-income poverty lines are now a good deal closer to these lines than in the past. Consequently, the share of national income needed to bridge that gap, to bring everyone up to these lines, is less.

In the context of poverty reduction it is not adequate simply to pursue policies to move people out of 'consistent poverty' (above relative-income poverty lines). While reducing the proportion of people in this category may be useful in terms of achieving arbitrarily chosen government targets, it does not address the critical issue of the adequacy of households or persons' incomes. In the context of the National Action Plan against Poverty and Social Exclusion (NAPincl) (cf. discussion below) targets focusing specifically on income adequacy are urgently required and necessary to ensure the plan's credibility. The National Anti-Poverty Strategy, published by government in 1997, adopted the following definition of poverty:

> *People are living in poverty if their income and resources (material, cultural and social) are so inadequate as to preclude them from having a standard of living that is regarded as acceptable by Irish society generally. As a result of inadequate income and resources people may be excluded and marginalised from participating in activities that are considered the norm for other people in society.*

This definition of poverty is, effectively, ignored by government when it focuses principally on reducing 'consistent poverty' and does not give priority to providing poor people with sufficient income to live life with dignity. This is a completely unacceptable situation that requires immediate change. Without adequate income, people will continue to live in poverty, irrespective of how their situation may be represented by government.

What does 'consistent' poverty mean?

Income, alone, does not tell the whole story concerning living standards and command over resources. As we have seen in the National Anti-Poverty Strategy definition of poverty, it is necessary to look more broadly at one's exclusion from the life of a society because of a lack of resources. This would involve looking at other areas where 'as a result of inadequate income and resources people may be excluded and marginalised from participating in activities that are considered the norm for other people in society'.

What are these activities? In seeking to answer this question, the ESRI, in various poverty studies, has measured people's access to 23 non-monetary indicators. These have subsequently been divided into three subsets, focusing on the basic dimension, the housing/services dimension and the secondary dimension. In the 'basic dimension' the indicators included by the ESRI are:

- A meal with meat, chicken or fish every second day
- A warm, waterproof overcoat
- Two pairs of strong shoes
- A roast joint of meat or its equivalent once a week
- New, not second-hand clothes
- Going without a substantial meal
- Going without heat
- Going into debt for ordinary living expenses.

Table 2: Percentage of households below the 50% income line and experiencing basic deprivation in 1994/1997/1998

	1994	1997	1998
50 per cent line	9.0	6.7	6.2

Source: Derived from Layte et al. (2001: 35)

The proportion of households experiencing income poverty who are also experiencing basic deprivation declined from 9 per cent in 1994 to 6.2 per cent in 1998. This percentage is likely to have fallen further in the period since then. While improvements in these figures are welcome, they should not be excessively praised. Simply, it is far more important to focus on removing people from the experience of poverty than to make them comfortable within it. Reductions in these figures are being identified as major success. Government claims to be tackling poverty effectively. However, these targets are limited in the context of the definition of poverty outlined above.

CORI Justice Commission considers this measurement of poverty to be insulting to poor people and to Irish society generally. This measurement is Dickensian in nature and was chosen arbitrarily by government as the basis for setting its income targets in the National Anti-Poverty Strategy.

Risk and Incidence of Poverty

When poverty is being analysed it is important to distinguish between the *risk* facing a particular type of household (i.e. the proportion of households of that type found to be in poverty) and the ***incidence*** of poverty (the proportion of all those in poverty who belong to that group).

Table 3 provides a breakdown, for the period 1973–98, of those below the 50 per cent poverty line (i.e. *incidence* of poverty), classifying them by the labour force status of the head of household.

- This shows that 60 per cent of households who experience poverty are households whose head is either on home duties (39.2 per cent) or retired (21.2 per cent).
- Households headed by an unemployed person make up the next largest group at 15.4 per cent.

Table 3: Composition of households under 50% relative poverty line by labour force status 1973–1998

	1973a	1980a	1987b	1994c	1997c	1998c
Employee	9.0	10.3	8.2	5.3	7.3	4.0
Self-employed	3.6	3.5	4.8	6.6	6.2	5.2
Farmer	26.0	25.9	23.7	8.0	5.0	6.2
Unemployed	9.6	14.7	37.4	30.3	18.9	15.4
Ill / Disabled	10.2	9.3	11.1	9.6	9.1	8.8
Retired	17.0	18.9	8.1	10.1	17.9	21.2
Home Duties	24.6	17.4	6.7	30.2	35.7	39.2
Total	100.0	100.0	100.0	100.0	100.0	100.0

Sources: Derived from Nolan and Callan (1996: 95) and Layte et al. (2001: 24)
Notes: a: Household Budget Survey Data   b: ESRI Data
  c: ESRI Living in Ireland Survey Data

The *risk* of poverty for each of these categories over the same 1973–98 period is outlined in Table 4.

- Table 4 shows that since 1997 the overall risk of poverty has increased further to 24.3 per cent.
- It also shows that the risk of poverty has increased for five out of the seven classifications. Households whose head is a farmer, unemployed, ill/disabled, retired or on home duties have all seen an increase in their risk of being exposed to poverty.
- Only households whose head is an employee or self-employed have experienced reduced risk.
- The risk of poverty has decreased dramatically since 1987 for households headed by a farmer. In the same period, however, the number of full-time farmers has decreased substantially.

Table 4: Risk of relative income poverty by labour force status 1973–1998 (50 % relative poverty line)

	1973a	1980a	1987b	1994c	1997c	1998c
Employee	3.9	3.7	3.5	2.8	4.0	2.3
Self-employed	10.1	8.6	10.5	15.1	17.1	15.8
Farmer	21.2	27.0	32.8	21.5	16.3	22.0
Unemployed	61.9	63.1	57.2	57.3	54.9	56.2
Ill /Disabled	42.8	48.2	33.7	50.0	60.4	72.6
Retired	29.5	23.3	9.1	10.2	23.3	28.7
Home Duties	42.2	32.2	9.8	33.2	48.6	58.4
Total	18.3	16.8	16.3	18.6	22.3	24.3

Sources: Derived from Nolan and Callan (1996: 96) and Layte et al. (2001: 24)
Notes: a: Household Budget Survey Data   b: ESRI Data
c: ESRI Living in Ireland Survey Data

Additional research on poverty risk by the ESRI has also identified:

- Between 1997 and 1998, the risk of falling below half average income rose for single-person households, notably where the head was aged 65 or over. In 1997, this risk was 40.1 per cent, and in 1998 it was 50.8 per cent. By 1998, single-adult households had become the highest risk group, with a risk figure more than twice that of the next highest group.
- The poverty risk attached to households of one adult with children also increased sharply between 1997 and 1998. These households now have a 42.4 per cent chance of experiencing poverty.

Children

The 1998 ESRI poverty data indicate a further decrease in the number of households with children who experience poverty. In 1994, households containing children accounted for 55 per cent of all households below the 50 per cent relative income poverty line; in 1998, this was 28 per cent. In general, between 1994 and 1998, there was a narrowing of the gap between the risks facing children and those facing adults. While this is clearly an improvement, the overall figure remains very high.

Gender

The 1998 ESRI poverty data clearly indicate that women in Ireland experience a greater risk of poverty than men. Table 5 outlines these trends and displays a gap between the percentage of men and women in poverty. This is particularly noticeable in the age group 65 and over. In that age group, 43.5 per cent of women are at risk of experiencing poverty, compared with 25.9 per cent of men. The greater dependency of elderly women on social welfare payments, whose growth has lagged behind average income growth, is a central part of the reason behind this trend.

As noted earlier, in Table 4, the 1998 data record an increased risk of poverty for single-adult households and households headed by someone working full-time in the home. Both these classifications comprise primarily households headed by women and help to explain further the growth in female poverty risk.

Table 5: Risk of relative income poverty by gender and adult's age 1994–1998 (50% relative poverty line)

	1994%		1997%		1998%	
	Men	Women	Men	Women	Men	Women
All Adults	14.5	16.7	15.5	21.6	16.8	22.2
Adults Aged 18–64	15.6	17.9	15.3	18.3	15.3	17.6
Adults Aged 65+	8.4	8.4	16.9	38.5	25.9	43.5

Source: Layte et al. (2001: 28)

Poverty Proofing

As part of the implementation of the National Anti-Poverty Strategy (NAPS) the social partners, including CORI Justice Commission, have been involved in a dialogue led by the Department of Social, Community and Family Affairs to develop mechanisms for poverty-proofing policies of government departments. A document was agreed that sets out how civil servants responsible for policy should assess policies for:

- impact on poverty
- contribution to achieving the NAPS targets
- ability to address inequalities leading to poverty

This is an important development that has the capacity to give a new direction to policy and the distribution of resources. A recent review by the National Economic and Social Council (NESC) has identified a number of areas within the existing poverty-proofing process that require improvement. It is clear that such improvements are necessary as, to date, the implementation of poverty proofing in areas such as the annual budget leaves a great deal to be desired.

How does Ireland compare with the EU on social protection expenditure?

The convergence of Irish incomes with the EU average has fuelled a growing expectation that Ireland should provide an EU level of services. One measure of such services is the level of social protection expenditure. Table 6 provides the most recently available figures for countries in the EU.

The percentage of GDP spent by Ireland on social protection continues to be lower than any other country in the EU, and it is decreasing. At 15.3 per cent of GDP, the Irish figure is more than 5 per cent smaller than the allocation in Portugal, the next lowest-spending country. Sweden, the country with the highest social-protection expenditure, spends more than twice as much as Ireland. While some of the difference may be explained by the fact that Ireland does not have as large a proportion of its population in the pension age group, the figures are still dramatic.

An Agenda for Fairness

Table 6: Social protection expenditure in the EU between 1996 and 1998 as a % of GDP

	1996	1997	1998
Belgium	28.8	28.5	26.9
Denmark	32.5	31.4	29.1
Germany	30.6	29.9	28.2
Greece	23.1	23.6	23.7
Spain	21.9	21.4	21.0
France	31.0	30.8	28.9
Ireland	18.5	17.5	15.3
Italy	25.3	25.9	24.3
Luxembourg	25.2	24.8	23.2
Netherlands	30.8	30.3	26.8
Austria	29.6	28.8	27.5
Portugal	21.6	22.5	20.4
Finland	32.3	29.9	26.4
Sweden	34.6	33.7	32.6
United Kingdom	27.7	26.8	26.0
EU-15	28.7	28.2	26.6

Source: Eurostat, February 2000 and September 2001.

It is clear that a larger proportion of Ireland's GDP could be spent on social protection. Increases to social welfare entitlements could facilitate the removal of every man, woman and child from income poverty and, even then, Ireland would still not be very high on this particular EU table.

An Examination of Low-Income Families
An examination by the Vincentian Partnership for Social Justice of the current social welfare and minimum wage rates underscores their inadequacy. The study concludes that, 'these rates do not reflect the

current cost of even the most frugal standard of living. There is an urgent need to increase them to a realistic level at which people can live with some dignity and without the burden of a continuous shortfall' (2001: 156).

The study was conducted during 2001 and involved 118 people in twelve community centres in seven parts of Dublin city completing a detailed questionnaire on their weekly income and expenditure. The study found that housekeeping and food were the most costly items for the majority of households, regardless of income. It also identified that people on social welfare experienced shortfalls because of the inadequacy of their income, rather than because of bad management of their income. The resulting financial pressure diverted family attention away from allocating enough time, commitment or money to areas such as education. Consequently, children may even leave school early to avoid further financial pressure on their parents.

Based on the survey and its findings, the Vincentian Partnership identified a number of key recommendations; these are (2001: 159–161):

- Raise the single adult social welfare rate to €184 (£145).
- Lone parents with two children need €254 (£200) a week to live life with some dignity.
- Increase child dependant allowance to a minimum of €25.40 (£20) a week for low-income families.
- Increase the provision of state-supported, affordable, childcare so that more people can avail of training and work opportunities.
- Encourage employers to adopt greater flexibility to working hours so that parents can work during school hours.
- Increase the back-to-school clothing and footwear allowance to a more realistic level.

How much better off are people under this Government?

Chart 1(a) seeks to discover how much better off people are following five budgets of the current Fianna Fáil/PD Government. In making these calculations, it is essential that wage increases be included, as well as tax cuts and social welfare increases. Unemployed people gain nothing from tax reductions or wage increases. Consequently, when assessing their position, it is essential that pay increases be included in the calculations.

We have included the wage increases contained in the national agreements *(Partnership 2000* and *The Programme for Prosperity and Fairness)* for the relevant years so that legitimate comparisons can be made. The numbers on Chart 1 are the gains over the full five years. Overall, it illustrates how much people's take-home incomes have increased over five budgets since the Fianna Fáil/PD Government came to power.

The outcome shows a dramatic widening of the rich/poor gap, as each of the five budgets gave substantially more to those who were better off than to those who were the poorest in Irish society. Single people who are long-term unemployed are £26 a week better off; those with incomes of £15,000 a year are £96 a week better off; while those on £40,000 are £206 a week better off.

After five budgets, couples who are long-term unemployed are £48 a week better off. Couples with one income earning £15,000 are £97 a week better off, while those on £40,000 are £190 a week better off. Over the same period, couples with two incomes earning a total of £15,000 a year are £107 a year better off, while those with two incomes totalling £40,000 are £263 a week better off.

The gap between rich and poor has now widened by £191 a week. In making these calculations, we have included pay increases, tax reductions, social welfare increases and the impact of the new savings scheme, which better off people can access, but which is beyond the reach of Ireland's poorest people.

Chart 1(a) shows that the disposable income of single people who are long-term unemployed and those on £40,000 a year has widened by £180 a week. The latter can also gain £11 a week from the new Government Savings Scheme, bringing their total gain up to £191 a week.

The impact of Government decisions on the take-home income of *couples* has been almost as striking. After five budgets, couples who are long-term unemployed are £48 a week better off, while couples on £40,000 are £190 a week better off. The latter also benefit from the Savings Scheme, so the gap between them has widened by £153 a week.

Widening the gap between the better off and the poor is unfair, unjust and bad for social cohesion. In making its decisions, Government has failed to honour the aims and objectives of the *Programme for Prosperity and Fairness*. These committed Government to building a fairer and more inclusive society.

Chart 1(a): How Much Better off are people under this Government (1997/2002)?

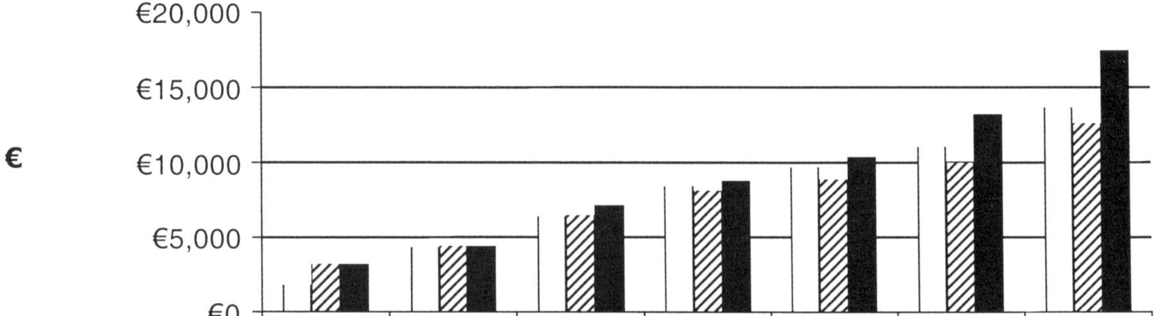

Gross	LTU**	€12697 £10000	€19046 £15000	€25395 £20000	€31743 £25000	€38092 £30000	€50790 £40000
Single	€1,742	€4,342	€6,410	€8,487	€9,722	€11,033	€13,660
Couple 1 Earner*	€3,213	€4,406	€6,477	€8,120	€8,904	€9,999	€12,62
Couple 2 Earners*	€3,213	€4,406	€7,137	€8,780	€10,372	€13,257	€17,468

* Except in LTU Case where there is no earner
** LTU: Long Term Unemployed

These Calculations include the impact of Budgets '98 to '02 and Partnership 2000 Phases 2,3 & 4 and PPF Phases 1,2 & 3.

2.4 National Action Plan against Poverty and Social Exclusion

In summer 2001, the Government submitted to the European Commission a National Action Plan against poverty and social exclusion (NAPincl). The four objectives of this new European programme are:

- To facilitate participation in employment, and access by all to resources, rights, goods and services.
- To prevent the risks of exclusion
- To help the most vulnerable
- To mobilise all relevant bodies.

In the years ahead, the NAPincl process should benefit from more ongoing engagement with similar approaches adopted across the EU. That process should also help to produce a meaningful set of anti-poverty indicators and targets and a greater emphasis on monitoring these indicators and targets in a coherent way.

Unfortunately, the plan submitted by Government raises serious questions concerning its credibility in tackling poverty and social exclusion. In effect, it is an insult to poor people. It fails to give priority to tackling the widening rich/poor gap; it lacks proposals of a scale required to address the healthcare and housing waiting lists; it contains no new initiatives or commitments to achieve the objectives agreed at the Nice meeting of heads of Government; and it does not contain any proposals to reduce the numbers living in relative income poverty. The plan also ignores the issue of asylum seekers, who are some of the most socially excluded people in Irish society. The issue of indicators to measure the progress of the action plan is also dealt with in a derisory way. Examples of 'suggested indicators which may be considered' are proposed, rather than providing a concrete list of indicators against which the plan may be judged.

Overall, the plan is a sad reflection on a Government with significant resources at its disposal, which fails completely to come to grips with the most pressing issues of poverty and social exclusion in Ireland today.

2.5 National Anti-Poverty Strategy Review 2002

The 2002 review of the National Anti-Poverty Strategy (NAPS), entitled *Building an Inclusive Society,* contains a major breakthrough on income adequacy. For the first time ever Government has decided to benchmark the lowest social welfare rates at 30% of gross average industrial earnings.

For years successive Governments have been challenged to ensure every man, woman and child was taken out of income poverty and had the resources necessary to live life with dignity. To achieve this, two initiatives were needed:
- The lowest social welfare rates had to be set at a level that would provide sufficient income to make that possible, and
- These rates had to be linked to an index that reflected the changing standard of living in the society.

CORI Justice Commission have constantly urged that these lowest social welfare rates be set at 30% of gross average industrial wages.

The key target on income set out in the review states that the lowest rates of social welfare will reach €150 a week in 2002 terms by 2007. In 2002 the sum of €150 is equivalent to 30% of Gross Average Industrial Earnings (GAIE). The actual amount of the lowest social welfare payments in 2007 will depend on the growth in average industrial earnings between now and then. In 2002 terms this means an increase from €118.80 to €150 a week for a single person on the lowest social welfare rate. In percentage terms this increase is in excess of 26%. This is a substantial commitment and we welcome it.

We also welcome the target to eliminate long-term unemployment as soon as circumstances permit but in any event not later than 2007. While the specific measures required to achieve this target are not included we welcome the setting of the target as it will set the context within which Government policy on this issue will be evaluated in the coming years.

Weaknesses

There are a number of major weaknesses in the review. *It "sets out the overall objectives, overall targets within the key areas and the arrangements to mobilise actions".* It is vague and/or very general in many areas and leaves a great deal to be decided in the course of the coming years.

In particular there is a lack of clarity on the status of the Framework Document published with the revised strategy. We welcome the Taoiseach's commitment expressed at the launch of the strategy that the specific policy initiatives outlined in the Framework Document will be implemented in the course of the coming years. If they are not implemented the new targets to which the Government is committing itself in the revised strategy will not be achieved in the stated time frame i.e. between now and 2007.

A rights-based approach

Finally, while we welcome the recognition of social, economic and cultural rights contained in the review, we are very disappointed at the narrow focus of the application of these rights in the remainder of the document.

2.6 Unemployment

The year 2001 witnessed the first significant increase in Irish unemployment rates since 1993. A minor increase of 0.1 per cent occurred in 1997; however, it was short-lived. At the end of 2000, unemployment, as measured by the Quarterly National Household Survey (QNHS), stood at a rate of 3.9 per cent (68,800 people), and by the year 2001, 79,500 people were classified as unemployed, giving an unemployment rate of 4.3 per cent (see Table 7). During 2001, unemployment dropped to 3.7 per cent, before the slowdown in the international and Irish economy began to have an impact.

Table 7: Labour Force changes 2000–2001

	Sept–Nov 2000	June–Aug 2001	Change
Labour Force	1,779,100	1,866,100	+87,000
In Employment	1,710,300	1,786,600	+76,300
Unemployed	68,800	79,500	+10,700
of whom LT Unemployed [a]	24,200	22,100	-2,100
Unemployment Rate	3.9%	4.3%	+0.4%
LT Unemployment Rate [a]	1.4%	1.2%	-0.2%

Source: QNHS November 2001, p14
Notes: a: LT = Long Term

A study of the profile of the individuals who became unemployed in late 2001 provides some interesting results. The predominant source of the newly unemployed is in the age groups 15–19 and 20–24. These age groups saw their unemployment rates increase from 8.25 to 11.2 per cent, and from 4.9 per cent to 7.2 per cent respectively. While some of these new-unemployed are likely to be accounted for by seasonal factors, such as third-level holidays, the scale of the increase is significant. In particular, included in the under 25s are early school-leavers who, with low skills, may find it difficult to get new employment given the economic conditions and the greater number of competing job-seekers. Depending on the extent of the economic slowdown, the potential for these individuals to become long-term unemployed must be monitored. In that context, predictions for 2002 are that unemployment will rise towards 4.7 per cent (ESRI, 2001).

Fall in the Level of Long-Term Unemployment

Of the 79,500 people unemployed in August 2001, 57,200 were unemployed for less than one year, while 22,100 were long-term unemployed. Long-term unemployment fell by 2,100 between the end of 2000 and August 2001. It should be noted that the level of long-term unemployment has consistently reduced since 1988, when it stood at 10.4 per cent, and that the major decline has been since 1996. The 2001 rate is only one-third of that recorded in mid-1998. This is a major decrease in the level of structural unemployment, and illustrates the extent to which Irish unemployment levels are now dominated by frictional factors. However, the return of cyclical unemployment in late 2001 and throughout 2002 underscores the necessity to maintain a focus on ensuring that the long-term unemployment problem is not allowed to return.

The one qualification needed here is to outline what the term 'unemployment' means. The QNHS unemployment data use the definition of 'unemployment' supplied by the International Labour Office (ILO). It lists as unemployed only those people who, in the week before the survey, were unemployed *and* available to take up a job *and* had taken specific steps in the preceding four weeks to find employment. Any person who was employed for at least *one hour* is classed as employed. By contrast, the live register includes part-time employees (those who work up to three days a week), seasonal and casual employees entitled to Unemployment Assistance or Benefit. The live register total for November 2001 was 154,100.

2.7 Income Distribution

As we have already outlined, poverty remains a significant problem, despite dramatic economic growth. The purpose of economic success is to improve the living standards of all of the population. A further loss of social cohesion will ensure that large numbers of people continue to experience deprivation, and the gap between them and the better off will widen. This has implications for all of society and not just for those who are poor.

Analysing the annual accounts of income and expenditure provides us with some information on trends in the distribution of national income. However, the limitations of this accounting system need to be acknowledged. Unpaid work is not included. Many environmental factors, such as the depletion of natural resources, are registered as income but are not seen as a cost. Pollution is not registered as a cost, but cleaning up after pollution is seen as income. Increased spending on prisons and security, which are a response to crime, are seen as increasing national income but are not registered as reducing human well-being.

The point is, of course, that national accounts do not include items that cannot easily be assigned a monetary value. Progress cannot be measured by economic growth alone. Many other factors are required, as we highlight elsewhere in this review. However, it is still of interest and of value to look at the distribution of national income. As we have acknowledged already, Ireland is doing very well when one uses the yardstick of economic growth as the basis of measurement. However, when judging economic performance, and making judgements about how well Ireland is really doing, it is important to look at the distribution of national income, as well as at its absolute amount.

Wage growth exceeded the growth in profits in 1991 and 1992, but the situation has been reversed since then. The moderate wage increases of recent years have been greatly exceeded by growth in output and profits. This picture becomes even more stark when the previously mentioned growth in employment is factored into the calculation.

Trends in Income Distribution among Households

It is useful in this context to focus on trends in income distribution among households in Ireland since the 1970s. A study by Collins and Kavanagh (1998) is most enlightening.

They tracked the level of inequality over the past two decades by examining the four Household Budget Surveys conducted by the

Central Statistics Office since 1973. Taking direct income as a measure, they found that the gap between the rich and the poor had increased significantly since 1973. They also found that the combination of tax and social welfare changes over that period had reduced this inequality somewhat, but disposable income remains highly concentrated at the top of the income distribution. They also showed that the growth in the economic cake, combined with the tax and welfare policies of governments, produced a situation in 1995 where the disposable income of the top 10 per cent of the population was greater than that of the bottom 50 per cent (24.67 per cent of all disposable income goes to the wealthiest 10 per cent, compared with 24.26 per cent to the bottom 50 per cent). The proportion of disposable income going to the bottom 50 per cent was the same in 1994 as it was in 1973 (see NESC Report No. 85 for the 1973 numbers). Consequently, all the tax and social welfare changes of more than two decades have simply maintained the proportion of disposable income going to the better-off half (i.e. 75.7 per cent) and to the poorer half of the population (i.e. 24.3 per cent).

The Widening Rich/Poor Gap

These trends in income distribution have been maintained throughout the late 1990s. The most recent data on income distribution, for 2000, are incorporated into Table 8. A commonly used measure of the scale of inequality is the ratio of the bottom 40 per cent's share of income to the top 20 per cent's share. The lower the ratio, the greater the degree of inequality.

Since 1995 the direct income of the bottom 40 per cent of households has increased. This can be explained by the aforementioned increases in employment and declines in unemployment. Many people in these households have gained direct income from wages. However, in spite of this increase, the allocation of direct income is such that the bottom 40 per cent have only 7.35 per cent of the total.

A more worrying trend is visible in the data for disposable income. There the percentage share of the bottom 40 per cent has declined while that of the top 20 per cent has increased. Consequently, the ratio has decreased to its lowest level ever for Ireland.

Table 8: The ratio of the bottom 40 per cent's share of household income to the top 20 per cent's share, 1973–2000

	Share of Highest 20%	Share of Lowest 40%	Ratio of the bottom 40% to top 20%
1973 Direct	46.97	11.04	0.23
1980 Direct	48.06	9.08	0.19
1987 Direct	52.54	6.04	0.11
1995 Direct	52.51	5.59	0.11
2000 Direct	50.85	7.35	0.14
1973 Disposable	42.09	17.36	0.41
1980 Disposable	40.13	17.36	0.43
1987 Disposable	40.97	17.54	0.43
1995 Disposable	41.34	16.62	0.40
2000 Disposable	42.68	15.62	0.36

Sources: Collins and Kavanagh (1998: 176) and Household Budget Survey Preliminary Results 2000.
Notes: Direct income is household income before taxation and transfers (before government intervention)
Disposable income is household income after taxation and transfers (after government intervention)

In the context of economic growth, the gap between rich and poor has further widened. Never before has the distribution of income in Ireland been so unequal.

2.8 Social Exclusion

Social exclusion results from a combination of deprivations. In particular, people experience exclusion when they live in poverty, cannot access employment, and do not have a say in the decisions that affect their lives. *Partnership 2000* described social exclusion as 'cumulative marginalisation: from production (unemployment), from consumption (income poverty), from social networks (community, family and neighbours), from decision making and from an adequate quality of life' (1996: 4.3).

Poor people are excluded from decision-making even when the decisions concern their level of income or their right to work. They are seen by many as a commodity, or are viewed as surplus to the requirements of society, and are dismissed accordingly. Society is now structured in such a way that people in these groups have no future prospects. Social and cultural life today requires money, and very often is organised around the place of employment. People who are poor and unemployed are excluded from the main life of the community.

Exclusion is experienced in many ways and can be multifarious. What does it mean if you are excluded? It means that your opinion is not sought and it doesn't count. In fact, you are not expected to have an opinion, rather you are encouraged to trust the opinion of the shapers and movers of the society. Ultimately, exclusion is not only the feeling, but also the reality of powerlessness.

When you are one of the excluded, politicians and policy-makers can ignore you without fear of censure or loss of position. When your rights are compromised, the avenues of redress open are very few and haphazard. Since society fears excluded groups, you are always suspect and live under a cloud of being guilty until you prove your innocence.

Observing the conspicuous consumption of the better off in the society while watching one's own children grow up without proper nourishment or access to appropriate education is demoralising. When these children begin to read reality for themselves, become disillusioned, and drop out of school, the cycle is complete. Another generation is added to the group of alienated and excluded.

People with a disability are, for the most part, among the excluded in our society. They and their families are expected to be grateful for whatever the rest of society decides to do for them. They have an inadequate voice in shaping the decisions that affect them.

The largest excluded group in Irish society is women. Since their exclusion is historically deep-seated and too complex for this publication, we can only acknowledge that it is experienced in various social, political, economic, cultural and religious areas. Exclusion is also experienced by ethnic groups, especially Travellers, and others because of their race, sexual orientation or religious beliefs.

A new excluded group in Irish society comprises refugees and asylum-seekers. In recent years, people of various ethnic origins have sought refuge here. For many of them, their experience of 'Irish hospitality' has not been good. It is ironic that a country which encouraged emigration as a way of solving our economic problems a mere decade ago (when an average of 35,000 people were leaving our shores annually) is now making life difficult for a substantially lower number of refugees and asylum seekers who have come here in recent years.

Exclusion is a concern not just of the excluded. When some of its members are not allowed to contribute or participate, all of society is poorer because it is deprived of the creativity, insights, skills and talents of the excluded members.

The involvement of the community and voluntary sector as a pillar of social partnership during the negotiations that produced the *Partnership 2000* and the *Programme for Prosperity and Fairness* (PPF) national agreements was a positive development. Issues of exclusion were given

Context

a greater priority than heretofore. *Partnership 2000* acknowledged that

> Social exclusion is one of the major challenges currently facing Irish society. To minimise or ignore this challenge would not only result in an increase in social polarisation, which is in itself unacceptable, but also an increase in all the attendant problems such as poor health, crime, drug abuse and alienation, which impose huge social and economic costs on our society.

Chapters dealing specifically with social inclusion and with equality formed part of that agreement. This was a major step in the right direction.

In its overview statement, the PPF agreement identified two of its four aims as to 'improve the quality of life and living standards for all' and 'to bring about a fairer and more inclusive Ireland'. Specific Frameworks were included in PPF to address Social Inclusion and Equality, Prosperity and Economic Inclusion and Successful Adaptation to Continuing Change. A far wider range of issues was addressed than had been the case in *Partnership 2000*. The latest agreement marked major progress compared to what had been achieved previously.

The commitment to supporting voluntary effort and the participation of the community and voluntary sector in the social partnership process in order to help combat social exclusion and disadvantage was continued in the PPF.

However, it has to be recognised that, to date, the group which has benefited least from the 'Celtic Tiger' is the excluded. Government has a unique opportunity now to redress this imbalance. CORI Justice Commission agrees with Mr Dermot Ahern, TD, Minister for Social, Community and Family Affairs, who said:

> *I feel very passionately that we're in a better position now than at anytime in our history to try to achieve a society where nobody feels left out. We mustn't forget that the economy is a means to an end, not an end in itself.... We've built an economy that's the envy of the world. Now, let's build a society that's the envy of the world in a new century* (Speech delivered at the opening of

CORI Justice Commission Conference on Social Partnership in a New Century).

So that this aspiration may become a reality, significant resources need to be invested in social inclusion programmes. Specifically, the commitments contained in the PPF agreement must be honoured.

2.9 An Agenda for Fairness

The sustained existence of all these problems, and outcomes, within Irish society, requires increased attention. It is necessary that society as a whole responds by adopting an agenda focused on achieving greater fairness. In the following pages, we outline what this agenda should entail. We address a range of issues including:

- Income
- Taxation
- Work
- Public Services
- Accommodation
- Healthcare
- Education
- Culture and Cultural Respect
- Participation
- Promoting Sustainability
- Rural Development
- Official Development Assistance

On each of these issues, we propose a core policy objective. We also provide an analysis of the present situation, review relevant initiatives from the National Anti-Poverty Strategy and outline policy proposals aimed at achieving greater inclusion and fairness. In doing this, we clearly indicate the choices CORI Justice Commission believes should be made when the available resources are divided in the years immediately ahead.

3. AN AGENDA FOR FAIRNESS

Objectives, Analysis and Policy Proposals

3.1 Income

> **CORE POLICY OBJECTIVE: INCOME**
> To provide all with sufficient income to live life with dignity. This would involve enough income to provide a minimum floor of social and economic resources in such a way as to ensure that no member of the national community falls below the threshold of social provision necessary to enable him or her to participate.

The sustained high rates of poverty and income inequality in Ireland require greater attention. Tackling poverty effectively is a multi-faceted task. It requires action on many fronts ranging from healthcare to education, from accommodation to employment. However, the most important requirement in tackling poverty is the provision of sufficient income to people to enable them to live life with dignity. No anti-poverty strategy can possibly achieve any success without an effective approach to addressing low incomes.

Budget 2002 failed to make any progress in addressing the issue of low income. Following its introduction, the poorest people in Irish society are expected to live on €118.80 (£93.56) a week. This sum is far from adequate, and those who receive it can expect to experience only the most frugal of living standards.

Calculating the impact of Budget 2002 across society reveals a further widening of the gap between rich and poor. Single people who are long-term unemployed gained €10.16 (£8) a week, those with €19,046 (£15,000) a year gained €19 (£15) a week while those on €50,789 (£40,000) are €41.90 (£33) a week better off. Couples who are long-term unemployed gained €20.32 (£16) a week. Couples with one income earning €19,046 (£15,000) became €21.59 (£17) a week better off, while those with an income of €50,789 (£40,000) became €34.28 (£27) a week better off. Finally, couples with two incomes earning a total of €19,046 (£15,000) a year gained €17.77 (£14) a week, while those with two incomes totalling €50,789 (£40,000) will receive €46.98 (£37) a week more.

Despite the failure of the recent budget to address low incomes, there has been some progress on benchmarking social welfare payments. In its final report, published in September 2001, the Social Welfare Benchmarking and Indexation Working Group agreed that the lowest social welfare rates should be benchmarked. A majority of the working group, which includes CORI Justice Commission, also agreed that this benchmark should be index-linked to society's standard of living as it grows, and that the benchmark should be reached by a definite date.

The working group chose Gross Average Industrial Earnings (GAIE) to be the index to which payments will be fixed. A majority agreed that the benchmark for social welfare payments by 2007 should be 27 per cent of GAIE. In 2002 terms this would mean that the lowest social welfare payment (at €118.80 [£93.57] a week) should be €138.85 (£109.35).

The CORI Justice Commission warmly welcomed these recommendations and believes that they marked 'a major breakthrough in the struggle to tackle poverty and social exclusion in Ireland'. If the recommendations are implemented, the lowest social welfare payment would rise dramatically, the target would be reached within a definite time frame, and social welfare payments would continue to increase in line with the improving living standards of the wider society.

CORI Justice Commission strongly urged Government to accept the recommendation to establish a benchmark for the lowest social welfare payments; this benchmark should be reached by 2007. The Community and Voluntary Pillar of Social Partners (including CORI Justice Commission) and the Trade Union Pillar both argue, and continue to argue, that the benchmark should be set at 30 per cent of GAIE, with the 27 per cent proposed acting as an interim target.

CORI Justice Commission believe that to do this would have a dramatic impact on reducing income poverty in Ireland and would go a long way towards removing the most fundamental cause of social exclusion. In accepting the GAIE index, the working group was following a precedent set by the Pensions Board, which had recommended that contributory old age pensions be benchmarked at 34 per cent of GAIE.

All members of the working group agreed that basic child income support (i.e. Child Benefit and Child Dependant Allowances combined) should be set at 33–35 per cent of the minimum adult payment rate. CORI Justice Commission, alongside representatives of the Community and Voluntary Pillar, offered qualified support to this position, citing concerns that the minimum adult rate must be set at an adequate level if the proposal is to be meaningful, and pointing to the need for renewed research on the costs of rearing children in order to inform the development of policy in this area. If the lowest social welfare payments were benchmarked at 27 per cent of GAIE, this would mean that by 2007 the basic child-income support would be in the range of €59–€63 (£47–£50) per week.

The majority of the working group who agreed to the recommendations included the Department of Social, Community and Family Affairs, the Community and Voluntary Pillar, the Trade Union Pillar and the Farming Pillar (i.e. three of the four pillars of social partners). The minority who dissented were the Department of Finance, the Department of Enterprise, Trade and Employment and IBEC (representing the employers' pillar of social partners).

National Anti-Poverty Strategy Review 2002
The NAPS Review 2002 set the following as key targets:
> To achieve a rate of €150 per week in 2002 terms for the lowest rates of social welfare to be met by 2007 and the appropriate equivalence level of basic child income support (i.e. child Benefit and Child Dependent Allowances combined) to be set at 33%-35% of the minimum adult social welfare payment rate.

CORI Justice Commission welcomes this target. It is a major breakthrough in social, economic and philosophical terms. The target of €150 a week is equivalent to 30% of Gross Average Industrial Earnings (GAIE) in 2002. This means that social welfare rates will be benchmarked to increases in average industrial wages from now on. It also means that the gap between the present level of the lowest social welfare payments and 30% of GAIE will be bridged between now and 2007.

We urged Government to set a target in the NAPS review that would ensure the lowest social welfare payment for a single person would reach 30% of Gross Average Industrial Earnings by 2007. Government has accepted our recommendation and we welcome this target as a major breakthrough in tackling relative income poverty in Ireland. We also welcome the commitment to ensuring that Child Benefit keeps pace with the increases in the lowest social welfare rates over the period to 2007. If this new target is honoured there will be a substantial reduction in the numbers of people living below the poverty line. We also welcome the commitment to monitor the proportion of the population falling below relative income poverty lines in line with the indicators agreed in the EU Joint Report on Social Inclusion.

However, we are concerned that the issue of low pay has not been addressed in the review. In particular we are disappointed that no commitment was made to make tax credits refundable as this is the most equitable tax instrument available to Government under the present tax system.

Policy Proposals

We have already seen that while the proportion of the population experiencing 'consistent poverty' has been declining, the number of people with incomes below the 50 per cent relative-income poverty line has been increasing. We have also seen that this level of income is very low and inadequate. A series of short-term and medium-term initiatives is required if the reality of poverty is to be addressed for once and for all in Ireland. These measures, which are necessary to bring about greater societal fairness, are outlined below.

- **Poverty-proof all public policy initiatives and provision.**
- **Equality-proof all public policy initiatives and provision.**
- **Increase child benefit substantially and do not tax it.**

There is widespread support for increasing child benefit if child poverty and family poverty are to be eliminated. It is also a very effective component in any strategy to improve equality. Child benefit remains a key route of tackling child poverty and is of particular benefit to those families on the lowest incomes. CORI Justice Commission, however, opposes the inclusion of child benefit as part of the parents' tax assessment.

- **Move towards individualisation of social welfare payments**

The issue of individualising payments, so that all recipients receive their own social welfare payments, has been on the policy agenda in Ireland and across the EU for several years. CORI Justice Commission welcomed the report of the Working Group, *Examining the Treatment of Married, Cohabiting and One-Parent Families Under the Tax and Social Welfare Codes*, which addressed some of the individualisation issues. More work needs to be done to progress this issue. The working group addressing this issue should be given greater priority in the policy development process.

- **Raise the 'qualifying adult' social welfare payments until they reach the single-adult payment rate**

CORI has previously recommended that there should be a move towards raising the 'qualifying adult' payments in the social welfare system to equal the payment received by a single adult. Recent budgets, including Budget 2002, have introduced increases in the 'qualifying adult' payments'. While these are welcome, progress towards equality should be speeded up.

- **Regularly update the list of indicators on which the number of people categorised as 'consistently poor' is based. The present list should be updated immediately**

The changing situation in society needs to be reflected in the list of indicators used in estimating the number of people who are 'consistently poor'.

- **Move decisively to implement the NAPS commitment that the lowest social welfare payment for a single person will be benchmarked to 30 per cent of GAIE by 2007**

Achieving this target would have a dramatic impact on reducing income poverty in Ireland and would go a long way towards removing the most fundamental cause of social exclusion.

- **Resource the production of up-to-date data in the area of poverty and social exclusion and ensure the publication of such data as soon as they become available**

The supply of data in the poverty and social exclusion area has improved in recent years. However, there is scope for substantial development to ensure that adequate data are available on income, healthcare, accommodation, education, etc. that can be disaggregated by social category and location. This work should be adequately resourced and the results published as soon as they become available.

- **Move towards introducing a basic-income system**

CORI's Justice Commission has argued, for a long time, that the present tax and social welfare systems should be integrated and reformed to make them more appropriate for the changing world of the twenty-first century. To this end, CORI has argued for the introduction of a basic-income system.

A basic income is an income that is unconditionally granted to every person on an individual basis, without any means test or work requirement. In a basic-income system, every person receives a weekly tax-free payment from the Exchequer, and all other personal income is taxed, usually at a single rate. For a person who is unemployed, the basic-income payment would replace income from social welfare. For a person who is employed, the basic-income payment would replace the tax-free allowance or tax credit in the income-tax system.

It is a form of minimum income guarantee that avoids many of the negative side effects inherent in social welfare payments. A basic income differs from other forms of income support in that:

- it is paid to individuals rather than households;
- it is paid irrespective of any income from other sources;
- it is paid without conditions. It does not require the performance of any work or the willingness to accept a job if offered one;
- it is always tax-free.

The recent *Report of the Working Group on Basic Income*, and its accompanying studies, show that basic income could be financed in the Irish context. CORI's work on implementation mechanisms has shown that a basic-income system could be implemented in practice. It is clear that the model proposed by CORI Justice Commission (i.e. a full basic income for all) can be implemented and can be financed without resorting to a too-high level of taxation.

There is real danger that the plight of large numbers of people excluded from the benefits of the Celtic Tiger economy will be ignored.

Images of rising tides and calm canals are no substitute for concrete policies to ensure that all are included. Irish society needs a radical approach to ensure the inclusion of all Irish people in the benefits of present economic growth. Basic income is such an approach.

Ten Reasons to Introduce Basic Income
- It is work and employment friendly.
- It eliminates poverty traps and unemployment traps.
- It promotes equity and ensures that everyone receives at least the poverty level of income.
- It spreads the burden of taxation more equitably.
- It treats men and women equally.
- It is simple and transparent.
- It is efficient in labour-market terms.
- It rewards types of work in the social economy that the market economy often ignores, e.g. household work, child-rearing, etc.
- It facilitates further education and training in the labour force.
- It faces up to the changes in the global economy.

3.2 Taxation

> **CORE POLICY OBJECTIVE: TAXATION**
> To collect sufficient taxes to ensure full participation in society for all, through a fair tax system in which those who have more, pay more, while those who have less, pay less

The issue of taxation is central to budget deliberations and to policy development at both macro and micro level. Consequently, it is crucial that clarity exist with regard to both objectives and instruments aimed at achieving these goals. To ensure the creation of a fairer and more equitable tax system, policy development in this area should adhere to the core policy objective outlined above.

The 2001 worldwide economic slowdown has had an impact on the Irish Government's taxation revenue. Based on a relatively high GDP growth prediction of 3.9 per cent for 2002, the Department of Finance (2002) has predicted a 2002 budget surplus of 0.7 per cent of GDP. Other economic commentators have suggested that Ireland will experience a budget deficit in 2002. However, all agree that, given the current structure of government spending and taxation, large deficits will be experienced from 2003 onwards.

This outcome provides a significant opportunity to whatever government takes office after the 2002 general election. Clearly, there is a requirement for a significant alteration to fiscal policy. CORI believes that a necessary inclusion in this alteration is a radical overhaul of the taxation and social welfare system in such a way as to meet our core policy objective. The first two budgets of any new administration should take the opportunity to widen the tax-base significantly and introduce greater equity to the system.

The remainder of this section outlines Ireland's relative taxation position, the impact of our proposals, the instruments available to government and some policy proposals.

Ireland's Total Tax Take

Ireland's total tax take is low by EU standards. In fact, according to Eurostat, the total tax take as a percentage of gross domestic product (GDP) is the lowest of fourteen countries for which statistics are available (see Table 9). Total tax and social insurance revenue in Ireland was equal to 34.1 per cent of GDP, a long way below the EU average of 42.6 per cent. Among the countries taking a higher percentage are Germany (41.6 per cent), France (46.3 per cent), Denmark (53.1 per cent), and the United Kingdom (35.9 per cent). As national wealth has grown in Ireland, there has since 1995 been a fall of more than 2 per cent, from 36.4 per cent, in the total government take from tax and social-insurance contributions.

Table 9: Taxes and Social Contributions as a % of GDP, 1997			
Sweden	54.1	Denmark	53.1
Finland	47.5	Belgium	46.6
France	46.3	Netherlands	45.9
Luxembourg	45.6	Austria	44.9
Italy	44.5	Germany	41.6
Portugal	37.9	Spain	36.2
UK	35.9	Ireland	34.1
EU 11 average	43.2	EU 15 average	42.6

Source: Eurostat

Because of the difference between GDP and GNP in Ireland, some argue that GNP is more accurate as a basis for comparison. When adjusted for this difference, however, Ireland's total tax take is still substantially below the EU average, and most EU countries take a far larger proportion of GNP in taxes and social levies.

The *Report of the European Commissioner for Economic Affairs* (2000) identified the existence of two alternative social models among EU member states. The report compared the effective rates of taxation on labour, capital and consumption among the member states, and identified two distinct social models within the EU member states.

Ireland, along with the UK, Spain and Portugal, were considered close to the US model, with taxes on labour of under 30 per cent. These countries favour competitiveness over social cohesion. A commitment to solidarity and social cohesion is evident in the tax policies of the Scandinavian countries that tax labour at 50 per cent, and in countries such as Austria, France and Germany which have rates of 40 per cent. The differences between these two models are based on fundamental philosophical differences concerning the redistribution of income and wealth through the tax and social welfare systems.

Both the Eurostat figures and the European Commission report underscore the identification of Ireland as a low-tax country.

Corporation Tax

Following Budget 2002, the standard rate of corporation tax was reduced from 20 per cent to 16 per cent at a full year cost of €347m. A further reduction to 12.5 per cent has been signalled for Budget 2003. These reductions are adding substantially to the high profits already enjoyed by the corporate sector. Following the 1998 announcement of the plan to reduce these corporate taxes, the Tánaiste and the Minister for Finance stated that the Government would 'examine in depth the scope for revenue yield from the business sector to ensure that the business sector will contribute an appropriate share of overall tax revenue' (Joint Statement, 22/7/98). They did not, however, specify what action they intended to take. Since then, no effective action appears to have been taken.

Serious questions remain, concerning the advisability of pursuing this policy approach. Windfall profits are flowing to a sector that is already extremely profitable. No evidence of substance exists to support the contention that corporations would leave if the corporate tax rate were higher — at 17.5 per cent, for example. While we accept that commitments entered into should be honoured, we strongly urge that a higher corporate tax rate form part of medium-term tax-policy strategy.

Income Tax

Impact of Income-Tax Changes in Budget 2002

A major anomaly in Budget 2002 was that the lowest paid did not benefit by a single cent from the income-tax changes contained in that budget. **Chart 1(b)** outlines the details. For example, a couple with one earner on £10,000 (€12,697) a year gained nothing from the budget tax and PRSI changes. Likewise, a couple with two earners on £15,000 (€19,046) a year gained nothing. At the same time, a couple with two earners receiving a total of £60,000 (€76,185) were €1,593 a year better off as a result of the tax and PRSI changes. This situation is unacceptable, unfair and unjust.

The instruments currently available to Government are so limited that this outcome will be repeated in the years ahead if a solution is not found. We suggest two possible solutions below, namely, make tax credits refundable or introduce a basic income system.

Income-Tax Change Options Open to Government within the Present System

There has been much discussion on how to target tax cuts at the lower-paid sector. As a basis for making choices within the present system, we produce here a simulation of the distribution of the benefits of tax cuts across a range of households of different sizes and different gross incomes. Our objective is to assess the distribution impacts of different tax instruments currently available to government. Each measure is examined in isolation and the changes in net income, compared with the situation for each household post Budget 2002, are assessed. The tax instruments examined are:

- **Chart 2:** Making the current tax credits refundable. The simulation clearly shows that all of the benefits from introducing such an instrument would go directly to those on the lowest gross incomes.
- **Chart 3:** Increasing tax credits by €100 per person. This instrument allocates resources equally to all categories of earners above €25,000. However, there is no benefit for those workers whose earnings are not in the tax net.
- **Chart 4:** Increasing tax credits by €100 per person and making this refundable. This simulation displays the equity attached to using the tax-credit instrument to distribute budgetary taxation changes. The benefit to all categories of income earners (single / couple, one-earner / couple, two-earners) is the same. Consequently, in relative terms, those earners at the bottom of the distribution do best.
- **Chart 5:** Reducing the standard tax rate by 1 per cent. Often this instrument is identified as a method of benefiting low earners. However, as the simulation shows, it is those on higher gross earnings who benefit most.
- **Chart 6:** Reducing the higher tax rate by 1 per cent. This instrument benefits only those earners at the upper end of the earnings distribution. No benefit flows to those earners on a gross income of less than €30,000; in fact, even those earners between €30,000 and €40,000 gain little.
- **Chart 7:** Widening tax bands by €1,000 per person. The impact of this instrument is that the primary gain goes to top earners. Those on low income gain little or nothing.
- **Chart 8:** Reducing PRSI by 1 per cent. Using this instrument, the effects are to benefit those with the highest gross earnings.
- **Chart 9:** Reducing the levy by 0.5 per cent. Introducing this tax policy would be of more benefit to those on higher gross income. The greater the income, the greater the gain.

Chart 1(b): *How much better off are people after the tax and PRSI changes in Budget 2002?*

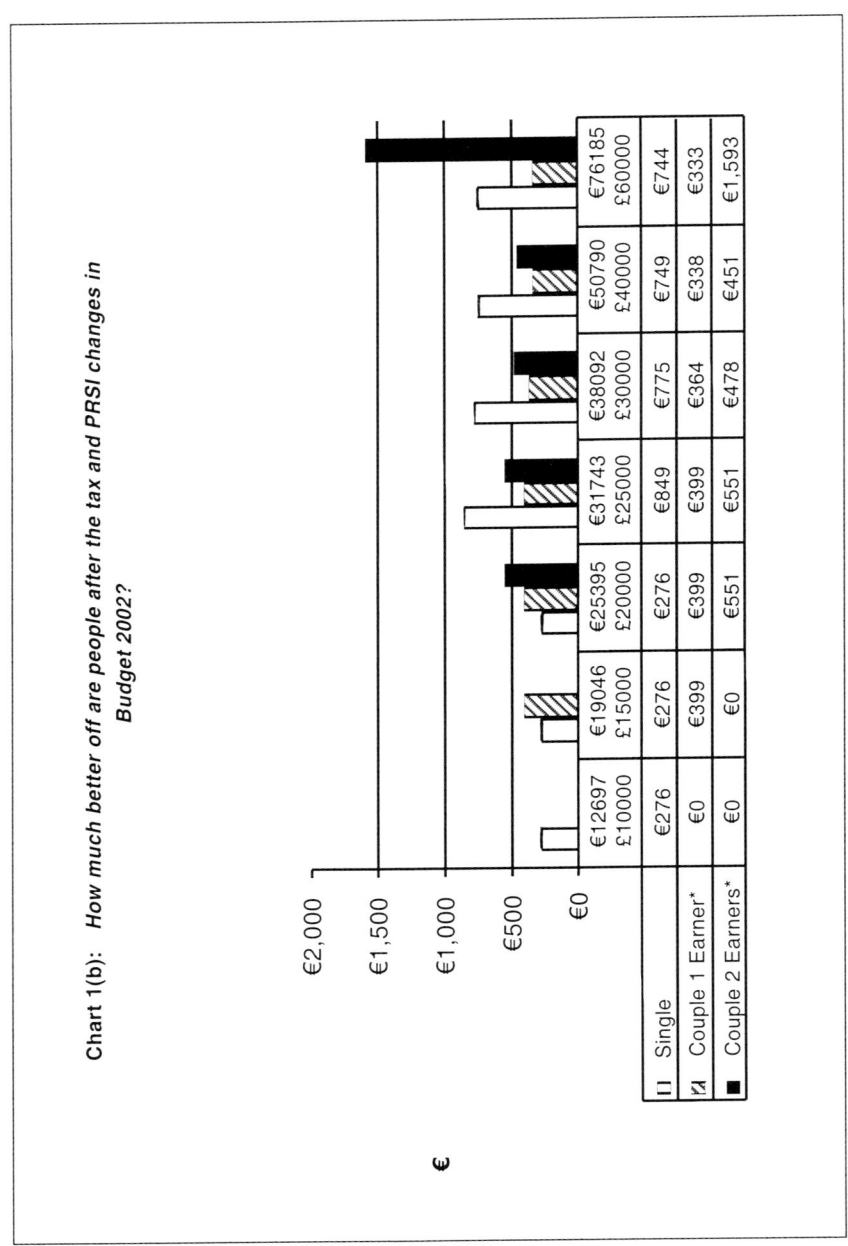

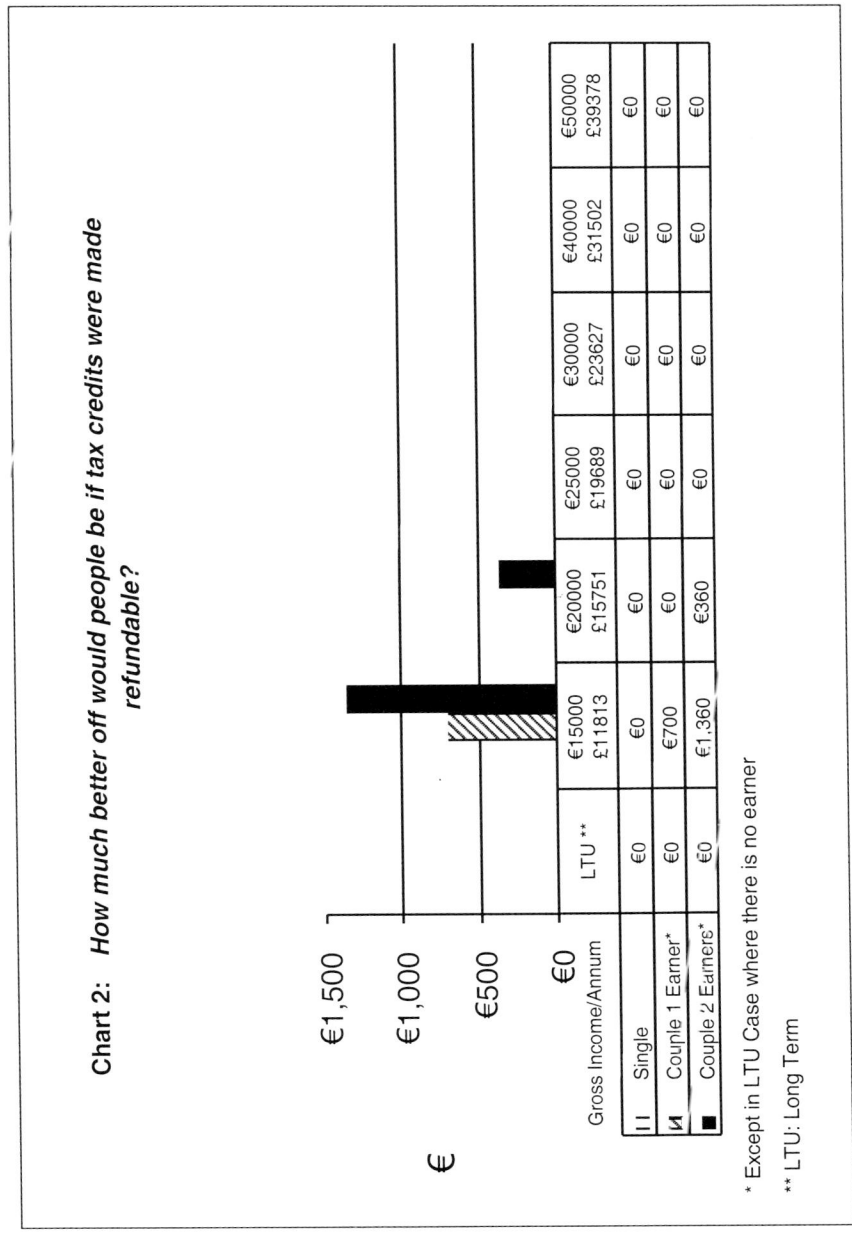

Chart 2: How much better off would people be if tax credits were made refundable?

Chart 3: How much better off would people be if tax credits increased by €100 per person?

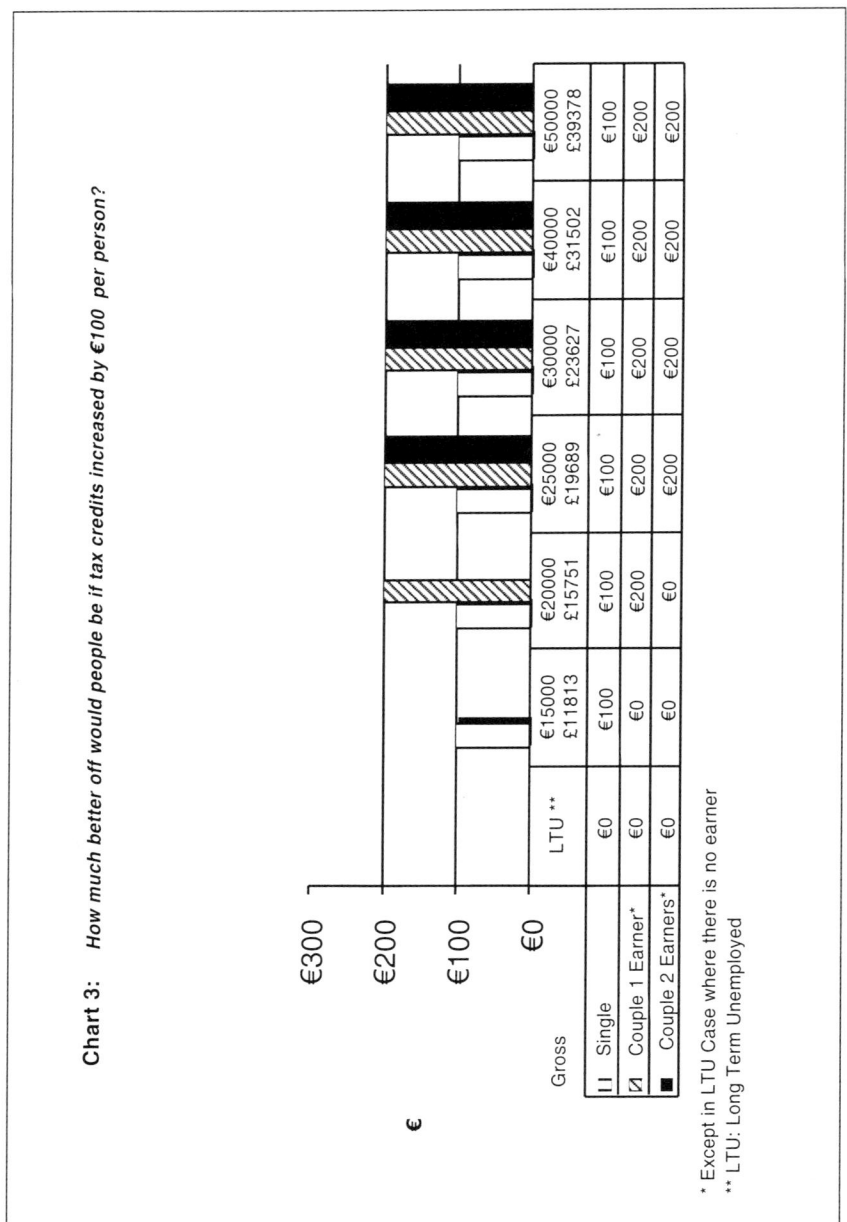

* Except in LTU Case where there is no earner
** LTU: Long Term Unemployed

Chart 4: How much better off would people be if tax credits increased by €100 per person and this was made refundable?

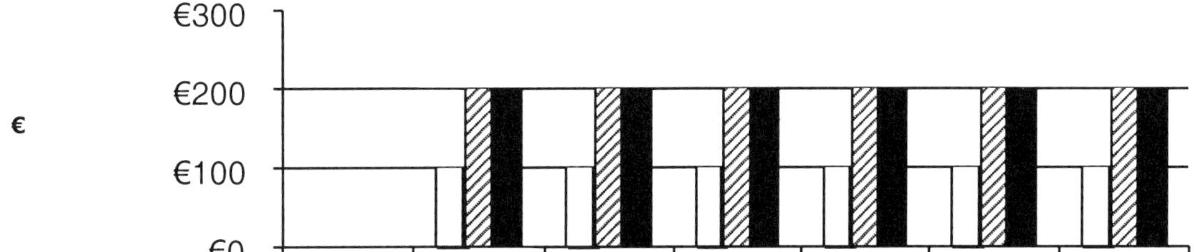

Gross	LTU**	€15000 £11813	€20000 £15751	€25000 £19689	€30000 £23627	€40000 £31502	€50000 £39378
Single	€0	€100	€100	€100	€100	€100	€100
Couple 1 Earner*	€0	€200	€200	€200	€200	€200	€200
Couple 2 Earners*	€0	€200	€200	€200	€200	€200	€200

* Except in LTU Case where there is no earner
** LTU: Long Term Unemployed

Chart 5: How much better off would people be if the standard tax rate was reduced by 1%?

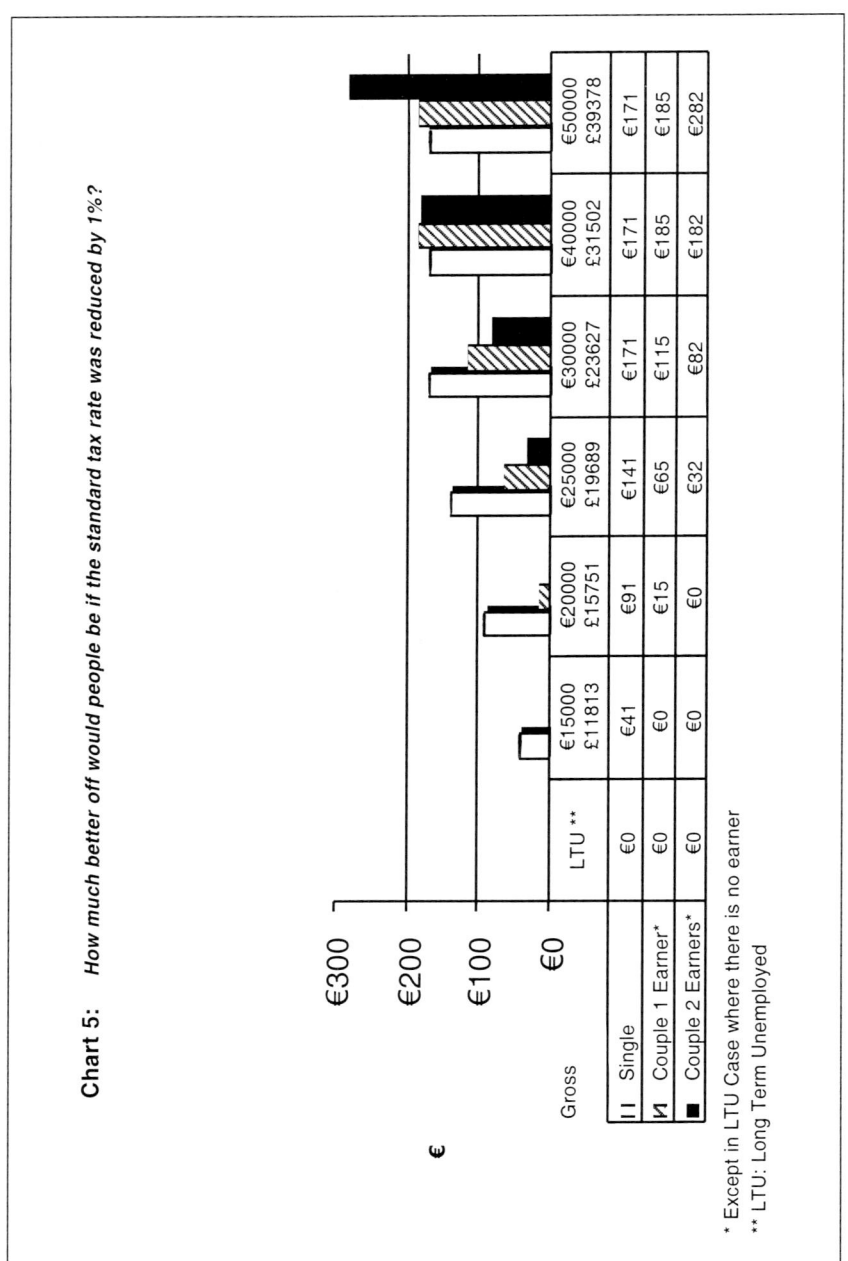

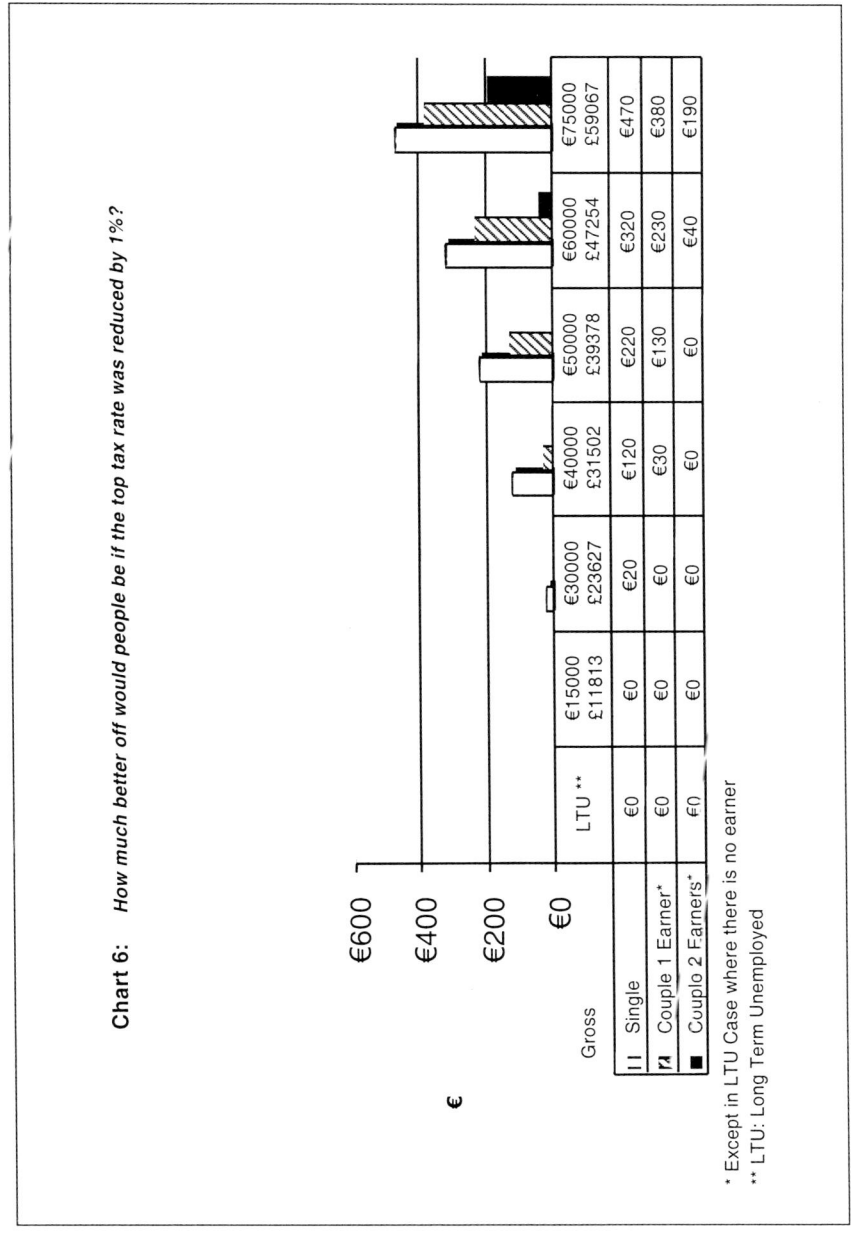

Chart 6: How much better off would people be if the top tax rate was reduced by 1%?

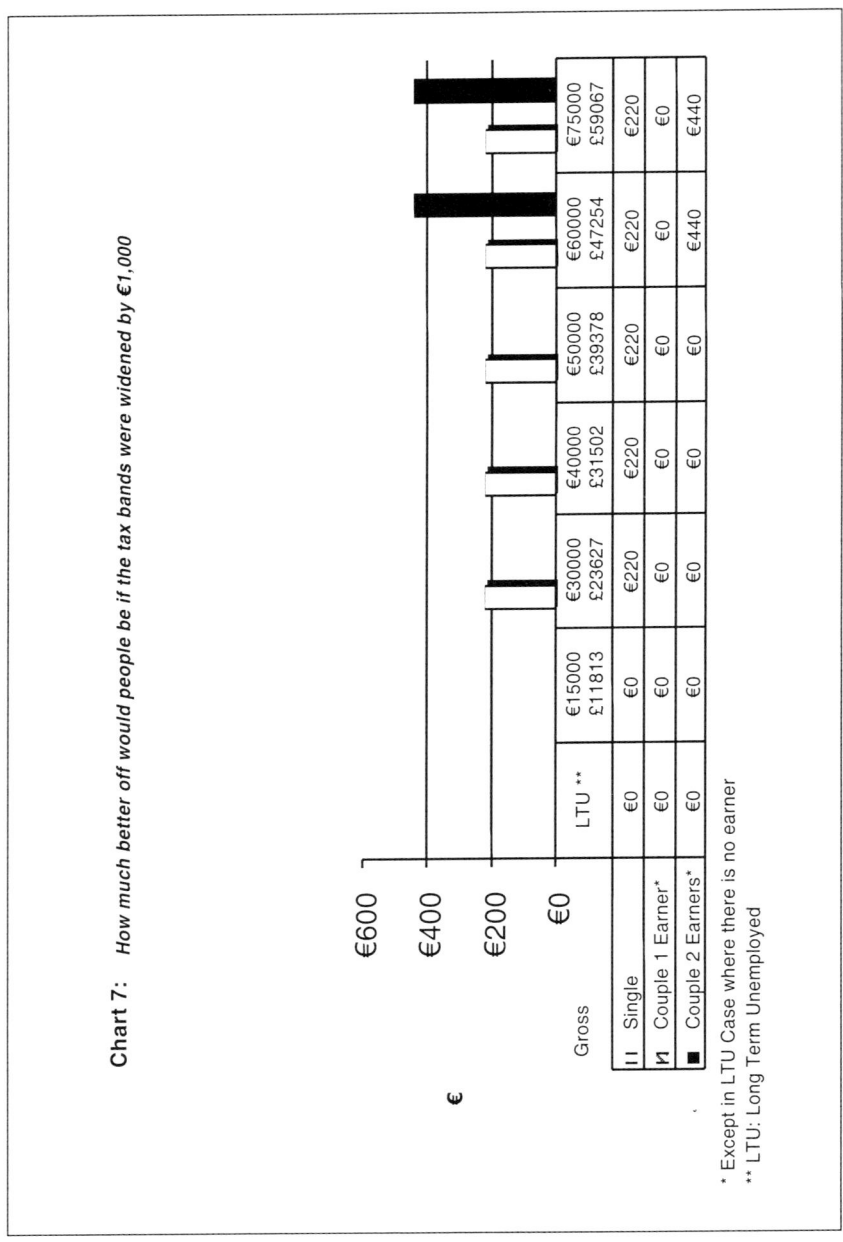

Chart 7: How much better off would people be if the tax bands were widened by €1,000

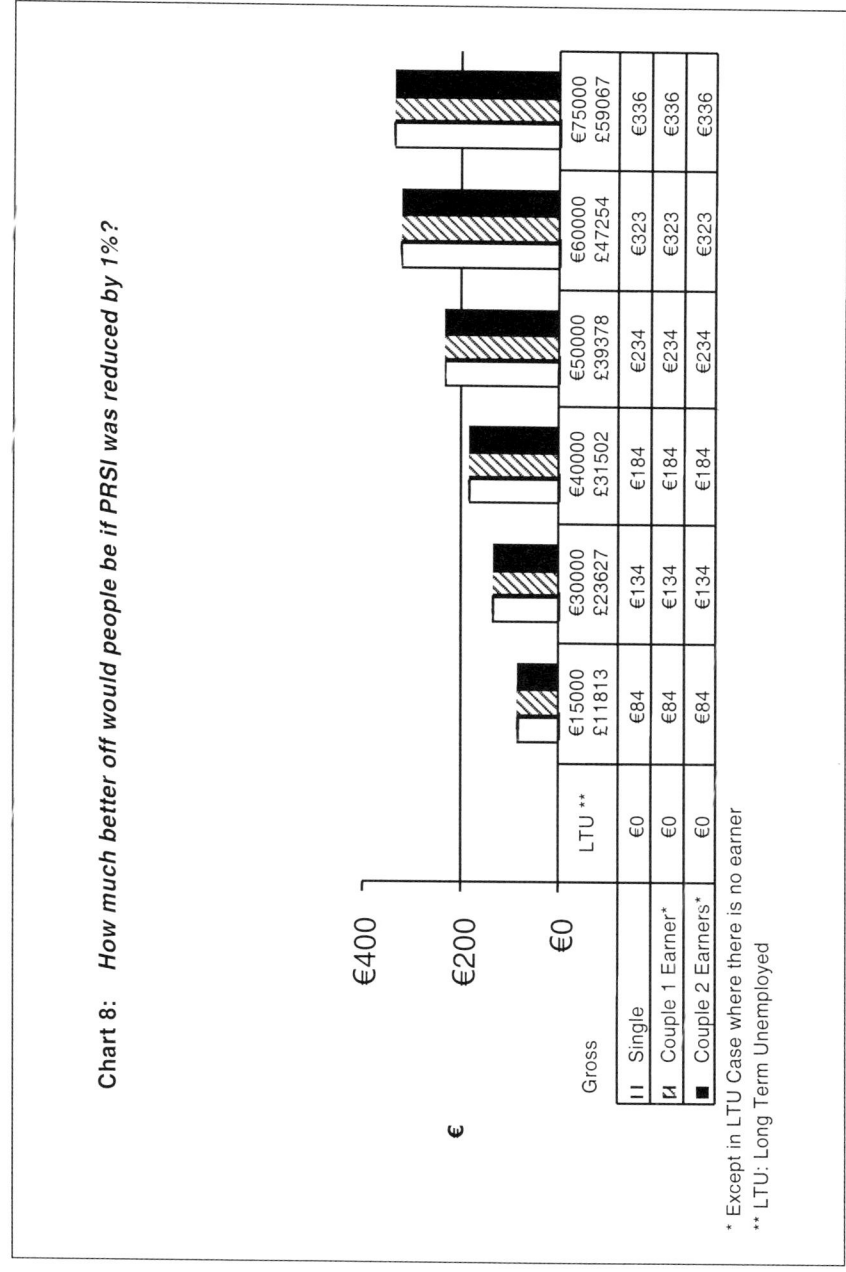

Chart 8: How much better off would people be if PRSI was reduced by 1%?

Socio-Economic Review 2002

Chart 9: How much better off would people be if Levy was reduced by 0.5%?

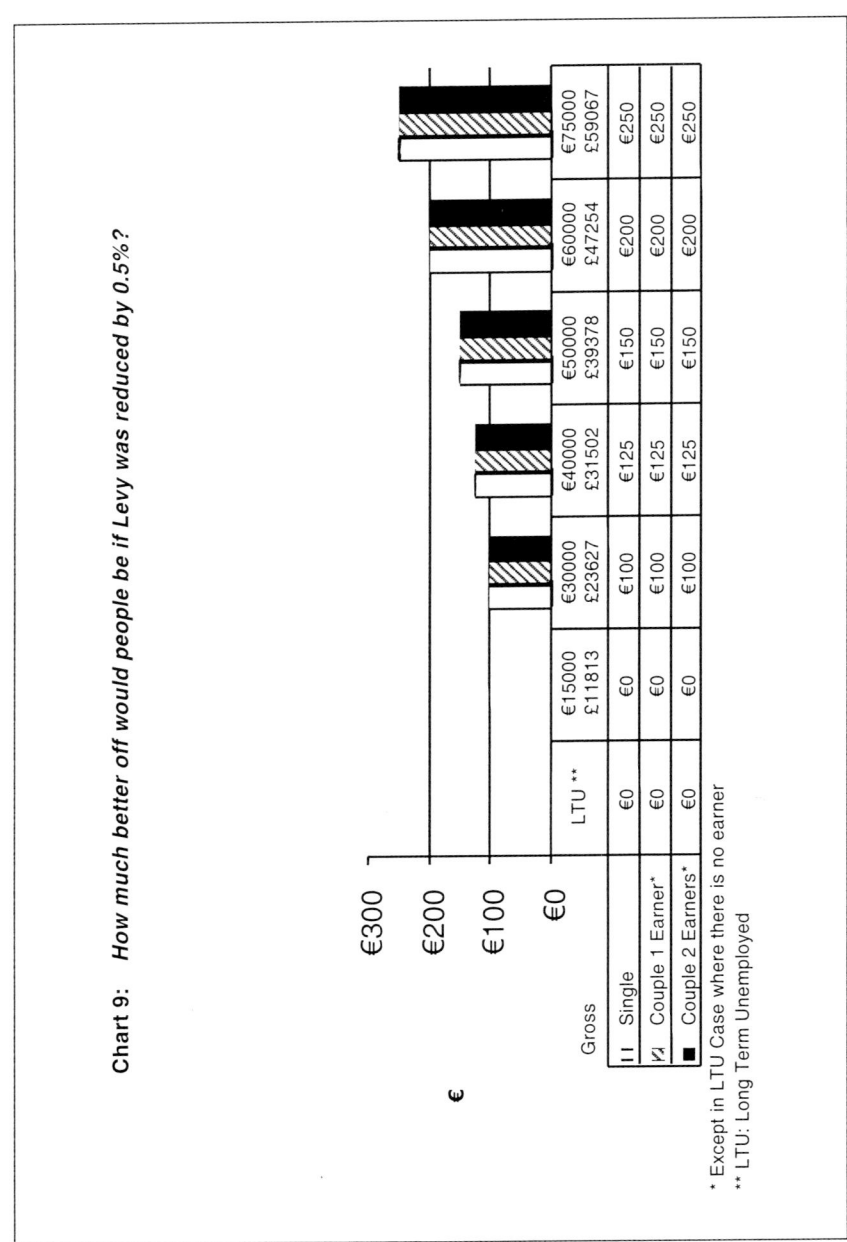

Gross	LTU**	€15000 £11813	€30000 £23627	€40000 £31502	€50000 £39378	€60000 £47254	€75000 £59067
Single	€0	€0	€100	€125	€150	€200	€250
Couple 1 Earner*	€0	€0	€100	€125	€150	€200	€250
Couple 2 Earners*	€0	€0	€100	€125	€150	€200	€250

* Except in LTU Case where there is no earner
** LTU: Long Term Unemployed

It can be seen from these simulations that few tax instruments have the capability of redistributing income to those who are lower paid. Almost all changes are regressive, in that they benefit the better off more than the low paid. This further widens the income gap between rich and poor. The one exception to this pattern is refundable tax credits (Charts 2, 3 and 4).

Refundable Tax Credits

Increasing tax credits, combined with standard rating of all discretionary tax allowances, provides government with a means of achieving greater equity among the top two-thirds of households in income terms (holding regular jobs on above €7,618 [£6,000] for a single person and €12,697 [£10,000] for a couple). However, tax credits would have to be made 'refundable' if low-paid employees were to benefit equally with the better off on Budget Day.

Currently, if a person does not earn enough income to use up their full tax credit, they will not benefit from any tax reductions. In effect, this means that the lowest-income earners in society do not benefit in any way at budget time. However, were tax credits to be made refundable, those whose tax bills are less than the credit would receive a payment equal to the difference.

The major advantage of making tax credits refundable would be in addressing the disincentives currently associated with low-paid employment. The main beneficiaries of refundable tax credits would be low-paid employees (full-time and part-time). Following the introduction of refundable tax credits, all subsequent increases in the level of the tax credit would be of equal value to all employees.

Basic Income is a Fairer System

The introduction of a basic-income system would be an even greater step towards genuine equality. It provides government with a very simple means of ensuring that every person — not just those in receipt of a taxable income — would benefit equally from budget changes. It has the added advantage in the present situation of being a far more progressive way of individualising the tax system. CORI's Justice Commission has, for many years, advocated the introduction of a basic-income system to replace the present tax and welfare systems.

Partnership 2000 included a section on basic income, which read:
> *A further independent appraisal of the concept of, and the full implication of introducing a basic income payment for all citizens will be undertaken, taking into account the work of the ESRI, CORI and the Expert Group on the Integration of Tax and Social Welfare and international research. A broadly based steering group will oversee the study.*

This work has been published and will act as a valuable support to the discussion on the government's Green Paper, *Basic Income*.

Individualisation
CORI Justice Commission has long supported the individualisation of the tax system. However, the process of individualisation followed by government is deeply flawed and unfair. The cost to the exchequer of this transition has been in excess of €0.75 billion, and almost all of this money has gone to the richest 30 per cent of the population. A significantly fairer process would have been to introduce a basic-income system that would have treated all people fairly and ensured that a windfall of this nature did not accrue to the best off in this society.

It is clear that, given the economic downturn, there will be an increase in the level of unemployment. Given the current form of individualisation, couples who see one partner lose his/her job will end up even worse off than they would have been had the current form of individualisation not been introduced.

Before individualisation was introduced, the standard-rate income-tax band was €35,553 (£28,000) for all couples. After that, they would start paying the higher rate of tax. Now, the standard-rate income-tax band for single-income couples is €37,000 (£29,140), while the band for dual-income couples is €56,000 (£44,104). If one spouse (of a couple previously earning two salaries) leaves a job voluntarily or through redundancy, the couple loses the value of the second tax band.

Indirect Taxes
In 2001, the Minister for Finance announced a 1 per cent reduction in the standard rate of VAT to 20 per cent. However, because of a failure to pass on this cut, the rate was restored to 21 per cent in Budget 2002. While the rate cut may not have been passed on, it is certain that the rate increase will be. Those who can least afford the resulting price increases will experience them most acutely.

Broadening the Tax Base
As outlined earlier, the likelihood of budget deficits from 2003 onwards and the relatively low tax profile of Ireland suggest a need to broaden the Irish tax base. As stated in our core objective, those who have more should pay more. We believe that there is merit in developing a tax package based on the realisation that it is better not to tax people and organisations on what they earn by their own useful work and enterprise, nor on the value they add nor on what they contribute to the common good. Rather, the tax that people and organisations should be required to pay should be based on value they subtract by their use of common resources. Therefore we suggest the introduction of two new types of taxation: (i) sustainability/eco taxes and (ii) land rent tax. A further tax is also proposed: (iii) taxes on financial speculation.

(i) Sustainability/Eco Taxes
Sustainable development is now a major issue. As the world has come to recognise that the supply of land, clean water and air etc. is not infinite, new questions emerge concerning sustainability. For example, as pressure mounts on the availability, not to mention the quality, of water on our planet, it is not simply environmentalists who warn us of impending disasters. Even institutions such as the World Bank are changing their approach to policy development to reflect this concern.

The finite nature of our environment demands that we take account of environmental costs along with other factor costs. Measures to protect the environment have necessarily involved intervention in the market, as the market forces do not themselves provide for environmental protection. Up to now this *intervention* has been by legislated regulatory measures.

In the long run, however, a more comprehensive approach is required. In recent years the sheer increase in the volume of economic activities has often negated regulatory gains. A key step would be to include in prices — and thereby internalise — the environmental costs occasioned by economic activity. It is difficult to devise any methodology capable of tracing and attributing with any accuracy all the costs/damage wrought upon the environment by a particular activity. Thus, in many cases, the internalisation can be achieved only in an arbitrary way, i.e. by taxes/charges based on broad national assessment.

(ii) Land Rent Taxes
This is a tax on the annual rental site value of land. The annual rental site value is the rental value which a particular piece of land would have if there were no buildings or improvements on it. It is the value of a site, as provided by nature and as affected for better or worse by the activities of the community at large. The tax falls on the annual value of land at the point where it enters into economic activity, before the application of capital and labour to it.

The arguments for a land-rent tax are to do with fairness and economic efficiency. Most of the reward of rising land values goes to those who own land, while most of the cost of the activities that create rising land values does not. This is because rising land values — for example, in prosperous city centres or prime agricultural areas — are largely created by the activities of the community as a whole and by government regulations and subsidies, while the higher value of each particular site is enjoyed by its owner.

This means that it often pays land owners to keep sites unused, in order to sell them later, when (they hope) land values will have risen. Speculation on rising land values distorts land prices, generally making them significantly higher than they would otherwise be.

In short, land-rent taxation would lead to more efficient land use within the structure of social, environmental and economic goals embodied in planning and other legislation (a more detailed assessment of the land-rent tax is provided in Robertson, 1994: 20–26).

(iii) Taxes on Financial Speculation

Global currency trading has been increasing dramatically as a result of the introduction of floating exchange-rate systems. It is estimated that 98 per cent of all financial transactions traded are speculative currency transactions. During the early 1990s this speculation resulted in a series of currency crises which had major implications for many developing countries where there was a decline in economic activity and a consequent increase in the levels of poverty. These speculative transactions are completely free of taxation.

There is growing support worldwide for the introduction of a tax on such speculative exchange transactions. The Tobin tax, proposed by the Nobel Prize winner, James Tobin, suggests that all speculative currency transactions be taxed at a rate of between 0.1 and 0.25 per cent. This would raise an estimated $150–$300 billion annually. It is proposed that the revenue generated by this tax be used for national social development and international development co-operation purposes.

In conclusion, we outline key policy proposals with regard to taxation.

Policy Proposals

- Make tax credits refundable.
- Increase tax credits substantially.
- Make Family Income Supplement (FIS) a part of the tax system.
- Proceed with individualisation in the income-tax system in a fair and equitable manner.
- Move towards a basic-income system.
- Ensure that changes in the income-tax system benefit those on low to middle incomes as much as they benefit the better off in cash terms.
- Accept a goal of having Ireland's total tax-take set at the EU average tax-take level.
- Poverty-proof all budget tax packages to ensure that tax changes do not further widen the gap between those with low income and the better off.
- Develop corporate tax initiatives to ensure that no windfall tax cut accrues to the corporate sector as a result of the dramatic reduction of the corporation tax rate towards 12.5 per cent.
- Increase the corporate tax rate in the medium term.
- Ensure that the distribution of all changes in indirect taxes discriminate positively in favour of those with lower incomes.
- Move decisively to shift the burden of taxation from income tax to eco-taxes on the consumption of water, fuel and fertilisers, as well as on the disposal of waste. In doing this, government should ensure that its impact on people with low incomes should not be negative.
- Investigate the possibility of introducing a tax on currency transactions such as the Tobin Tax.
- Investigate the possibility of introducing a land-rent tax. This, and the preceding proposal, could lead to substantial reductions in income tax.

3.3 Work

> **CORE POLICY OBJECTIVE: WORK**
> To ensure that all people have access to meaningful work

As we have already noted, one of the major achievements of recent years has been the increase in employment and the reduction in unemployment, especially long-term unemployment. In 1991, there were 1,156,000 people employed in Ireland. Ten years later, this number had increased by more than half a million to 1,786,600. Over the same period, the number of people unemployed (measured on an ILO basis) had gone from 198,500 to 79,500. In the intervening years, the number unemployed had exceeded 220,000.

While this transformation is remarkable, it does provides new challenges and raises new questions.

The Challenge of Unemployment

The issue of unemployment remains a challenge and is likely to be more problematic in the year ahead as further job losses appear. It is necessary that the Government should make provision for this new situation by emphasising and providing additional resources to prepare and enable unemployed people to access jobs. This should involve providing additional resources to support education and retraining, expanded opportunities for work-place experience and adequate numbers of places on programmes such as Community Employment.

The Importance of Balance

The new situation created by the huge growth in available jobs raises major questions concerning the focus of policy in this area. Should Ireland continue to expend resources to increase further the number of jobs available? Given the problems being experienced in trying to increase the labour supply (by recruiting women, older people and people from abroad), should more emphasis be placed on improving the quality of jobs available, and the education, training and life-long learning capacity of people in the labour force? The latter approach seems more sensible.

The Need to Recognise All Work

A major question being raised by the current labour-market situation concerns assumptions underpinning culture and policy making in this area. One such assumption concerns the priority given to paid employment over other forms of work. Most people recognise that a person can work very hard even though they do not have a job. Much of the work done in the community and in the voluntary sector fits under this heading. So too does much of the work done in the home. The need to recognise such work has been acknowledged in the Government's White Paper, *Supporting Voluntary Activity*. Higher priority should be given to this issue within policy making. CORI Justice Commission support for the introduction of a basic-income system comes, in part, from a belief that all work should be recognised and supported.

Impact of a Basic Income on the Labour Market

Clark and Kavanagh (1995) investigated the possible impact of the CORI Basic Income proposals on the Irish labour market. They concluded that our proposals:

- would not adversely affect the efficiency of the Irish economy or reduce the level of output;
- would reduce the female, youth and elderly components of the labour force by between 20,000 and 40,000;
- would generate small increases in employment in the short run;
- would reduce the unemployment rate by 2.4 per cent;
- could increase employment in the long-run;
- would not lead to a downward adjustment in wages;
- would not address the issue of low pay directly;
- would be a first step in the move towards a post-industrial definition of work and labour.

Clark and Kavanagh concluded their paper by stating, *'There are strong economic and social arguments in favour of a Basic Income, not the least of which is its role in changing the structure of the labour market in the 21st century'.*

National Anti-Poverty Strategy Review 2002
The NAPS Review 2002 set the following as key targets:
> **To eliminate long-term unemployment as soon as circumstances permit but in any event not later than 2007. To reduce the level of unemployment experienced by vulnerable groups towards the national average by 2007. To achieve the objectives set out in the National Employment Action Plan to increase employment rates.**

CORI Justice Commission welcome the target to eliminate long-term unemployment and we urge Government to make every effort to ensure that this target be achieved by 2003 as stated in the Framework Document. We also welcome the commitment to reduce the level of unemployment experienced by vulnerable groups towards the national average. However, specific targets and indicators are required to ensure this target is met.

We are very disappointed that the Government rejected the proposal to recognise the right to work of asylum seekers. We, along with others such as the Irish Refugee Council, advocated that where Government fails to meet its own stated objective of processing asylum applications in six months the right to work should be granted to asylum seekers. Clearly recognition of such a right would alleviate poverty and social exclusion among one of Ireland's most vulnerable groups.

In conclusion, we outline key policy proposals with regard to work.

Policy Proposals

- Seek at all times to ensure that new jobs have reasonable pay rates.
- Develop employment-friendly income-tax policies which ensure that no unemployment traps exist. Policies should ease the transition from unemployment to employment.
- Place an ongoing emphasis on preparing and enabling unemployed people to access market-place jobs. Such an emphasis would involve:
  - increased numbers of places providing quality education and training, retraining and up-skilling;
  - expanded opportunities for unemployed people to gain work-place experience;
  - adequate numbers of places on programmes such as Community Employment.
- Maintain a sufficient number of active labour-market programme (ALMP) places available to those who are long-term unemployed.
- When ALMPs are mainstreamed, particularly in disadvantaged areas, ensure that sufficient resources are made available to maintain the services that were provided.

The education/training allowances available on programmes such as Community Employment are very low, bearing in mind the training needs of the target groups. Increases in these have been recommended in various reviews. The PPF contains a commitment that spending on programmes will move towards training in order to reflect better the needs of both the market and the individual.

- Increase the education/training grants for participants on Community Employment, Job Initiative and Rate for the Job programmes, and seek accreditation for all education/training and all work done by participants in these programmes.

- Expand the social economy programme. We believe that there is an urgent need to fund this programme on the basis of the service provided, as was originally intended

- Increase grants, to community and voluntary organisations providing services, to reflect national agreements, especially in the area of wages.

- Recognise the right to work of all asylum seekers whose application for asylum is at least six months old (and who are now entitled to take up employment).

- Develop a programme providing a 'one face, one place' service for refugees and asylum seekers, which would promote the integration of these groups into the labour market.

- Recognise work that is not paid employment. Everybody has a right to work, i.e. to contribute to his or her own development and that of the community and the wider society. This, however, should not be confined to job creation. *Work* and a *job* are not the same thing.

A great many people work very hard even though they do not have a job. The work they do is worthwhile and contributes to the development of society, their community or themselves. Yet their contribution to society is very often not recognised.

A more comprehensive approach is required which moves society towards recognising and rewarding work other than paid employment.

- Conduct an annual survey to discover the value of all unpaid work in the country (including community and voluntary work and work in the home). Publish the results of this survey as soon as they become available.

3.4 Public Services

> **CORE POLICY OBJECTIVE: PUBLIC SERVICES**
> To ensure the provision of, and access to, a level of public services regarded as acceptable by Irish society generally

Increasingly, Ireland is being identified as a country whose public services are underdeveloped. Given the wealth of the economy, this is a situation that is far from acceptable. As poorer people rely on public services more than those who are better off, it is they who are most acutely affected by this shortage.

We address public services over this section, and the next three sections on accommodation, healthcare and education. This section assesses public transport, library services, information technology and sports facilities.

Public Transport
Transport remains a most problematic area. Bottlenecks throughout the country are adding to the difficulty, and cost, experienced by everybody in conducting their lives. The sustained increase in the number of cars is also adding to problems of environmental destruction.

A new transport policy would seek to combine easy access, affordable and high-quality public transport with the high costs of ownership and use of private vehicles. The failure to give adequate resources to some of the national rail services raises serious questions about government commitment to the environment and to rural and peripheral areas.

Library Services
The new structures established under the reform of local government have the potential to renew local democracy and local development. One of the objectives of the *Programme for Prosperity and Fairness* is:

to provide a continuum of education provision from early childhood to third level targeted at tackling educational disadvantage and promoting equality of opportunity and participation.

Central to these developments is information and easy access to this information. Coupled with information is the need for easy access to modern means of communication. Libraries are obvious centres with potential to support these objectives. To play this potential role, expansion of the library service is essential.

Information Technology

Increasingly, the ability to use information technology (IT) is becoming a central requirement in modern society. The phenomenon of a technological divide is becoming evident. In particular, it is of concern that a number of young people, including early school-leavers, have little or no skill in IT. As we have seen earlier, these are the people now becoming unemployed, and therefore their return to employment will be hampered by their relatively poor skills. Initiatives are necessary to improve IT provision in schools, as well as to increase its availability in areas such as public libraries and community centres. To date, the CAIT initiative by the Department of Public Enterprise has been successful in addressing these problems and achieving a large response. More schemes such as this are required.

Sports Facilities

Recent studies indicate a declining level of participation by Irish people, and in particular young people, in sports activities. Long term, this may have significant health consequences. There is a special case to be made for poor areas, most of which have limited, if any, sports facilities. The National Sports Council has introduced a creative initiative of local sports partnerships. Some of these are working effectively already and attempting to address this problem. However, the refusal by government to expand the funding for local sports partnerships is leaving a huge potential untapped. Clearly, this policy needs to change.

Policy Proposals
- Target funding strategies to ensure that far greater priority is given to providing an easy-access, affordable and high-quality public transport system.
- Provide substantial additional resources for the development of library services throughout the country.
- Increase the provision of open-access information technology in public libraries.
- Adopt further information-technology programmes to increase the skills of schoolchildren, early school-leavers and the unemployed.
- Provide additional funding to the Sports Partnership initiative.

3.5 Accommodation

> **CORE POLICY OBJECTIVE: ACCOMMODATION**
> To ensure that adequate accommodation is available for all citizens and to develop an equitable system for allocating resources within the housing sector

Housing and Accommodation Policy

A comparison of European housing tenures illustrates the existence of three main models of housing provision: an owner-occupier sector, a rental sector and a social housing sector. Most countries have a mix of housing tenures that reflects the policy choices of government. Irish housing policy supports owner occupation to the detriment of all other forms of housing tenure.

Ireland's level of home ownership reflects the high value Irish people put on owning their own homes. It also reflects public policy which provides a variety of tax incentives to those who have the resources to invest in housing. Since the 1970s, it has been the policy of successive Irish governments to subsidise owner occupation heavily. This has been achieved by the abolition of local rates on residential property and the subsequent failure to implement a system of residential property tax. More recently, investment policies have been introduced that favour investment in residential development. Investors in urban renewal schemes stand to gain over 419 per cent on their investment (Bacon, 1998). These policy developments, combined with policies of mortgage-interest tax relief, cash grants to first-time buyers, and very favourable tenant purchase schemes, have resulted in an extremely high level of home ownership. Owner-occupiers make up 79.3 per cent of the Irish population — this is considerably higher than the EU average of 56 per cent. Government housing policy has resulted in a housing system that is not tenure neutral and which has led to the residualisation of the rental sector, both public and private.

The down-the-line effect of this policy is the lack of availability of adequate accommodation for larger and larger numbers of households. The value of home ownership should be discussed in the light of present realities. These include: the increasing prices paid for houses and for land rezoned for housing; the burden of mortgage repayments especially on young families; the ghettoisation of local authority housing because private owners object to developments which may seem to devalue their properties; difficulties in providing suitable accommodation for special groups, e.g., Travellers, homeless people, asylum-seekers, young offenders, drug abusers, etc.

Housing Crisis

During the 1990s, improved levels of economic growth, combined with low interest rates, have resulted in high levels of housing inflation. This, in turn, has resulted in a crisis in housing provision in both the public and the private sectors. In the private sector, this crisis is evident from the rapid increase in house prices and from the severe difficulties experienced by first-time buyers seeking affordable houses. In the public sector, the demand (waiting lists) for public housing has increased substantially in the past five years at a time when house building in the public sector has been at a very low level.

Social Housing

In Ireland, the social-housing sector is the sector that provides housing for those on low incomes. The Department of Environment and Local Government defines social housing needs as *'the housing needs of households whose resources are insufficient to provide them with access to suitable and adequate housing'* (1995: 5). Based on this definition, social housing needs are met by the local-authority rental housing sector, voluntary housing schemes and, increasingly by subsidising the private rental sector through the Supplementary Welfare Allowance (SWA) rental-subsidy scheme. This definition fails to take into account the very significant state subsidies provided to the owner-occupied sector through mortgage-interest tax relief; the discounted local authority tenant purchase schemes or the shared-ownership scheme, all of which could be regarded as having a social component.

In the context of the present level of housing need, the definition of social housing should be broadened to encompass all areas of state subsidy to the housing sector.

Housing Needs

According to Threshold, at the end of 2001 there were an estimated 58,789 households on local-authority housing waiting lists. This figure represents a growth rate of 114 per cent since 1996, and indicates that about 140,000 people are in need of accommodation (Threshold, 2001 and Focus Ireland, 2002).

Table 10: The Need for and Supply of Local Authority (LA) Social Housing, 1996–2001a

	Households on LA Waiting Lists	Stock of LA Housing Unit	Waiting List as % of Rental Stock
1996	27,427	98,394	28
1999	39,176	99,163	40
2001a	58,789	101,657	58

Source: Threshold, 2001: 1
Notes: a: 2001 figures are estimates

Concurrent with this growth in waiting lists has been minimal growth in the provision of local-authority social housing. The overall stock has increased by only 3,263 units or 3.3 per cent. It is little surprise, therefore, that local-authority waiting lists are increasing substantially.

A recent survey by Focus Ireland (2002) identified that a number of local authorities, including those in Waterford, Westmeath, Monaghan and South Cork, all experienced a doubling in size of their housing lists between November 2000 and November 2001. From the perspective of vulnerable households, it is becoming more difficult to get a local-authority house. Single people are also disadvantaged on housing lists because most current housing developments are for families. Time spent on the waiting list is getting longer as is the waiting list itself. Rents continue to rise in the private rented sector, even though house prices have stabilised. Little progress has been made in advancing the Traveller Accommodation programme. Homelessness is obviously a growing problem.

An Agenda for Fairness

These figures once again raise questions about progress and who has benefited from the 'Celtic Tiger'. Notably, they do not include a significant number of people who do not qualify for a place on a local-authority housing list but still cannot afford to buy or even rent accommodation at current market prices. Future assessments of housing need must take account of new demands for accommodation and should include information on the following categories:

- people on local-authority waiting lists;
- people no longer able to buy affordable housing;
- new job-seekers from abroad;
- homeless persons;
- refugees and asylum-seekers.

House Completions

Table 11 shows the rate of house completions in the various sectors between 1995 and 2000. There was a 7 per cent increase in house completions during 2000, marking a slowdown from the record 9.8 per cent achieved in 1999.

Table 11: House Completions, 1995–2000				
Year	Local Authority Housing	Voluntary/Non Profit Housing	Private Housing	Total
1995	2,960	1,011	26,604	30,575
1996	2,676	917	30,132	33,725
1997	2,632	756	35,454	38,842
1998	2,771	485	39,093	42,349
1999	2,909	579	43,024	46,512
2000	2,204	951	46,657	49,812

Source: Annual Housing Statistics Bulletin, 2000. Department of Environment and Local Government.

The vast majority (93 per cent) of houses completed were built by the private sector. Local authorities built only 2,204 houses in 2000, a decrease of 705 on 1999. However, during 2001, there has been some improvement in the local-authority housing programmes. Threshold (2001) estimates that the 2001 figure for local-authority housing output will be 5,000, more than double the 2000 figure. This growth is in line with commitments given by government in the National Development Plan, and is a welcome improvement. A further growth to 6,000 new units is predicted for 2002. However, in spite of this progress, the overall situation remains far from acceptable.

Table 12: Local Authority Completions and Acquisitions, 1995–2000			
	Local Authority Completions	Local Authority Acquisitions	Total
1995	2,960	882	3,842
1996	2,676	897	3,573
1997	2,632	585	3,217
1998	2,771	511	3,282
1999	2,909	804	3,713
2000	2,204	1,003	3,207

Source: Annual Housing Statistics Bulletin, Department of Environment and Local Government.

Table 12 further shows the depth of the housing crisis. At a time of such need, the total number of LA completions and acquisitions is only 3,207. Furthermore, it is of concern that this total figure is decreasing.

It seems likely that the additional units provided in 2002 (via completion and acquisition) will do nothing other than meet the additional demands on local-authority housing that appear during the year. Clearly, additional government investment in local-authority housing is necessary.

The Private Rented Sector

A recent study of the private rental sector points out the circular and complex links between the structure and operation of the housing system and poverty and social exclusion (McCashin, 2000).

The private rented sector is the *'tenure of last resort for those unable to obtain local authority housing or not yet ready to enter owner-occupation'* (McCashin, 2000: 43). Traditionally, the private rental sector was the residual sector of the Irish housing system. It was characterised by poor-quality accommodation and non-secure tenure at the lower end of the housing market. The percentage of the population dependent on this sector to meet their housing needs declined from 17.2 per cent in 1961 to 8 per cent in 1991 (Department of Environment and Local Government). This compares with an EU average of 21 per cent (Commission of the European Communities).

The composition of the sector changed dramatically during the 1990s. A combination of a growing population, changing household structure, and the increasing cost of owner-occupation has seen the number of households in the private rented sector increase by more than 60 per cent, accounting for 11 per cent of households. It is estimated that there were 131,000 households living in this sector in 1997. Of these, 80 per cent were under 35 years of age and 58.2 per cent were single (McCashin, 2000).

Today, this sector is highly differentiated, with high-quality housing and relatively secure tenure at the upper end of the market, and low-quality housing and insecurity of tenure at the lower end. Both ends of the market have experienced dramatic increases in rent over this period.

At the lower end of the market, an increasing number of households are in receipt of Supplementary Welfare Allowance rent supplement. The number of households dependent on rent supplement has increased from 33,000 households in 1995 to 42,683 in 2000. Of those in receipt of rent supplements, 42.6 per cent live in the Eastern Health

Board Region (ERHA), and 56 per cent were aged between 20 and 34 years of age (Department of Social, Community and Family Affairs, 2001).

The Housing (Miscellaneous Provisions) (1992) Act provided for the registration of private rental properties. All landlords were required to register their rented properties with the local authority. It is estimated that over 130,000 households live in private rented housing. To date, just over 20 per cent of these houses have been registered, and, upon inspection, many have been found inadequate. Of the dwellings inspected in the Dublin Corporation area in 1998, 72.4 per cent did not meet the requirements of the regulations.

The Act requires certain minimum standards that could be inspected at any time. The low compliance with the Act and the inertia to implement it suggest that households accommodated in this sector are not a priority for government. This is very worrying given that the health boards spent over €150m (£119m) in 2000 to finance the accommodation of 42,683 households in this sector (Department of Social, Community and Family Affairs, 2001). This means that taxpayers are often subsidising poor-quality, but expensive, accommodation to the benefit of unregistered landlords.

Homelessness

It is possible to extract from the assessment of housing needs information about those most urgently in need of accommodation — the homeless. The most recent data, from 1999, show that the level of homelessness has risen from 2,501 in 1996 to 5,234 in 1999, an increase of 109 per cent. The 5,234 homeless persons comprise 2,593 adult men, 1,399 adult women and 1,399 children. These figures include those who have nowhere to sleep at night, along with those sleeping in hostels and other Health Board accommodation. Focus Ireland has suggested that in late 2001 the number of homeless had further risen to 6,000. Recent media reports have highlighted the increase in the number of homeless young people sleeping rough on the streets. The plight of these neglected children sleeping in doorways contrasts sharply with an economy in which million-pound property sales are no longer uncommon.

A study undertaken for the Homeless Initiative (1999) provides a more comprehensive picture of the extent of homelessness in the Dublin region. In March 1999, this survey found 2,900 adults with 900 dependent children homeless in the counties of Dublin, Wicklow and Kildare. Over 50 per cent of those surveyed had been homeless for more than a year and 14 per cent had been homeless for the previous five years. In the week prior to the survey, 275 of those surveyed had slept on the streets, 1,102 had spent the week in a hostel, 426 were in bed and breakfast accommodation, 44 were in a refuge, and 667 were staying with friends because they had nowhere else to go.

These statistics illustrate very clearly the complex and diverse nature of homelessness. Research has shown that there are three broad categories of homeless people. The first category consists of those who become homeless because of poverty combined with either eviction or a relationship breakdown. The second and growing category of homeless persons consists of those who have chronic disabilities or special needs as a result of alcoholism, mental illness or drug dependency. This group has multiple needs, of which housing is just one (Homeless Initiative, 1999). A third category of homeless persons has emerged in Ireland in recent years — this comprises asylum-seekers and refugees who have specific housing and other social-service needs.

The Homeless Initiative points out that homelessness is part of the continuum of housing need. It recommends a 'continuum of care' approach to the provision of services to homeless people. The objective of this approach is to address the needs of homeless people humanely, to enable them to move to appropriate permanent housing and to attain long-term economic and social stability. Consequently' the Initiative proposed the setting up of a Homeless Services Support Centre in the Eastern Health Board region.

The Forum on Youth Homeless established by the Eastern Health Board in 1999 reported in April 2000. The most significant finding of this forum was the lack of co-ordination among the numerous agencies attempting to deal with this problem. Financial and other resources are necessary to solve the problem of youth homelessness. However, the key recommendation of the Forum was the establishment of a single independent statutory authority with responsibility for developing and delivering services in this area.

The increasing level of homelessness is a shocking indictment of the failure of public policy and the lack of social concern for one of the most disadvantaged groups in Irish society. However, the number of homeless people is small relative to current economic resources and could be dealt with quickly if given the appropriate level of resources, political commitment and institutional structures. An independent national agency is required to oversee and implement a national policy on homelessness.

Gradually, progress is being made in this area. Budget 2002 allocated €10m specifically to implement the Youth Homeless Strategy and to develop care and protection initiatives. This is a welcome step forward, but much more needs to be done.

Policy Response to the Housing Crisis

The Government responded to the crisis in the owner-occupier sector by attempting to address the issues of supply and affordability of private houses for first-time buyers. It commissioned three reports (Bacon, 1998, 1999, 2000), and implemented the majority of the recommendations contained in them.

These recommendations have ranged from policies:
- to increase the supply of land for private housing;
- to shorten the planning process;
- to restrict Section 23 tax relief for investor landlords;
- to require builders to provide 20 per cent of building land for social housing;

- to increase residential densities;
- to revise the rates of stamp duty payable by investors;
- to introduce an anti-speculative property tax.

While the Government acted promptly to attempt to address the problems that emerged in the private housing sector, it paid relatively little attention to the problems that have been building up in the public housing sector over a much longer period of time.
The report of the National Economic and Social Forum (NESF) project team on 'Social and Affordable Housing and Accommodation' stands as a welcome review of this area. It also contained some excellent policy proposals which should be acted upon. Principal among these is the proposal to establish a National Housing Authority. This is a proposal with which we strongly agree, but whose establishment has still failed to materialise.

Government policy has failed to address housing as a system consisting of a number of inter-related tenures. The sectoral nature of the terms of reference of recent studies has led to policy fragmentation and sets of recommendations for one sector that have potential negative implications for other housing tenures. Policy co-ordination is clearly required.

National Anti-Poverty Strategy Review 2002
The NAPS Review 2002 set the following as key targets:
> **To ensure that housing supply is brought more into line with demand.**
> **To deliver 41,500 local authority housing unit starts (including acquisitions) between 2000 and 2006.**
> **To deliver an appropriate mix of social and affordable housing measures.**
> **To establish appropriate targets in light of the information gathered in the March 2002 statutory assessment of housing needs.**

Accommodation

> **By end 2004, sufficient and appropriate emergency accommodation and outreach services to be available to rough sleepers. This will be revised at end 2003 if necessary.**

CORI Justice Commission believe that the targets stated above on housing and accommodation fail to provide added value to existing commitments. While the next statutory assessment on housing needs (to take place in March 2002) will provide useful data for setting targets, present figures estimate over 50,000 households in need of local authority housing. Given the scale of the need the response is totally inadequate.

The target to deliver on 41,500 local authority unit starts (including acquisitions) between 2000 and 2006 will do little to tackle the growing number of households on local authority waiting lists.

The Framework Document contains a number of targets and proposed actions. Targets regarding housing standards should be improved i.e. damp and inadequate heating conditions should be eliminated by 2007 and not reduced by 50% as stated in the document. The provision of local authority housing and accommodation should be such that the maximum length of time 90% of households are on waiting lists would fall to 18 months by 2004, to 12 months by 2007 and to 6 months by 2010. An additional target is required in order to avoid a situation where length of time on waiting lists becomes the only criteria for being offered housing or accommodation. A balancing objective is required for households in priority need for example, those households accepted as in priority groups, including those homeless, will have their long-term housing needs met within 6 months by 2004.

We welcome the commitment in the Framework Document that a pilot initiative will be established by June 2002 to facilitate the development of sustainable indicators.

Policy Proposals

- Adopt an integrated analysis of the current housing and accommodation crisis and develop a housing and accommodation policy to address equitably the issues of supply and affordability of housing and accommodation for those in all housing and accommodation tenures. This should be done under the aegis of the Housing Forum established under the PPF.
- Set up a National Housing Authority.
- Revise the definition of social housing and identify a comprehensive range of social-housing policy objectives to meet the diverse housing needs of the Irish population. This task should be assigned to the PPF Housing Forum.
- Set up an independent national agency to oversee and implement a national policy on homelessness.
- Provide sufficient resources to eliminate homelessness by 2003.
- Broaden the definition of social housing and formulate a radical and diverse range of social-housing initiatives to meet the needs of those in all housing tenures.
- Continue to increase the budget allocation for local authority and voluntary/non-profit housing.
- At the very least, meet the commitment in the National Development Plan (2000–2006) to an annual output of 10,200 units of social housing.
- Ensure the realisation of the requirement that 20 per cent of building land be allocated for social housing.
- Develop and support policies focused on mixed housing, mixed communities, choice of tenure, and mix of different-sized housing units.
- Provide new resources for the security and management of local-authority housing.

- Actively implement and enforce the 1992 legislation with respect to the private rented sector of housing.
- Set a target of reducing to a maximum of six months the time spent on waiting lists — to be achieved by 2007.
- Provide the resources required to ensure implementation of the Travellers Accommodation programme.
- Give a special focus to tackling issues concerning accommodation for homeless people, refugees and asylum-seekers.

3.6 Healthcare[1]

> **CORE POLICY OBJECTIVE: HEALTHCARE**
> To provide an adequate healthcare service focused on enabling people to attain the World Health Organisation's definition of health as a *state of complete physical, mental and social well-being and not merely the absence of disease or infirmity*

Healthcare is a social right that every citizen should enjoy. Citizens should be assured that care is guaranteed in their times of vulnerability. The standard of care is relative to the resources and expectations of the society. The obligation to provide the right to healthcare rests on all citizens. In a democratic society, this obligation is transferred through the taxation and insurance systems to governments and other bodies who assume/contract this responsibility. The commitment of successive governments to the provision of healthcare as a social right to all citizens must be questioned in the context of a service that:

- has a public hospital waiting list in excess of 24,000 (December 2001 figures);
- has one of the lowest levels of doctors per head of population in the EU;
- has a major shortage of nursing staff.

Poverty and Health Status

The link between poverty and ill health has been well established by international research. The poor get sick more often and die younger than those in the higher socio-economic groups. Poverty directly affects the incidence of ill health; it limits access to affordable health and reduces the opportunity for those living in poverty to adopt healthy lifestyles. Health exclusion is a major dimension of poverty and social exclusion.

---

[1] *The Justice Commission acknowledge the work done by CORI Healthcare Commission in preparing this section.*

Health Policy

Key principles 2001: equity, people-centredness, equality and accountability.
Quality and Fairness: A Health System for You, 2001

Key principles 1994: equity, equality and accountability.
Shaping a Healthier Future, 1994.

In November 2001, the Government published a National Healthcare Strategy for the continued development of the Irish health services. This strategy, entitled *Quality and Fairness: A Health System for You*, was developed after consultation with both consumers and service providers. The strategy has four key principles, namely, equity, people-centredness, equality and accountability.

Three of these principles were also the basis of the last national health strategy of 1994, entitled *Shaping a Healthier Future*. Yet, inequality increased during this period as waiting lists became longer, and the commitment to the development of the community sector was not fulfilled. Where this strategy differs is that it sees six main frameworks for change, and one of the key factors of this change would be the primary-care sector. To support this, a strategy entitled *Primary Care: A New Direction* was launched.

Each framework is supported by dedicated actions with a time frame commitment. This is indeed a very welcome development. The problem would be that the strategy itself would appear to continue to sustain a two-tier system — that is, a public service that is tax funded, and a private insurance system. This has been shown to have increased the inequality in the system, yet the strategy does not change the basis of the health system.

The launching of *Primary Care: A New Direction* as part of the strategy gives a commitment to the development of a model of primary care based on the Alma-Ata definition of primary healthcare, recognising that health is much broader than disease and any one profession. Primary care is seen as the development of good working relationships between all professional team members in the field. However, there was no mention of the community health voluntary worker as having a part to play in the development of these teams.

The document places a very strong emphasis on the need to develop and educate professionals, but does not put any emphasis on the development of the community so that its members can be enabled take the responsibility, which is theirs, for their health which the strategy supports.

> *A health system that supports and empowers you, your family and community to achieve your full health potential.*
> *Quality and Fairness: A Health System for You, 2001*

To ensure the development of *Primary Care: A New Direction,* it is necessary to shift the healthcare budget's emphasis away from a central focus on hospital care towards community care. A balance must be struck between the funding provided for high-tech/acute care and community care. World Health Organisation (WHO) policy, agreed in 1972, set out to shift the emphasis to community care. For the WHO policy to work, there must be a more realistic shift in emphasis to community care, with a corresponding transfer of government resources.

To enable this to occur it will be necessary to:
- educate the public about the benefits of having a local health service and encourage them to use it, and support them when they do;
- place emphasis on preventative healthcare;
- encourage hospital consultants to work in the community;
- make special provision for people who are geographically or socially excluded;

- research, pilot and evaluate alternative initiatives in the delivery of healthcare.

A serious effort needs to be made to commence this process in 2002. In recent years, policy initiatives to de-institutionalise services, especially with regard to the care of people with mental disability, the care of the elderly and aftercare have been expedited on the assumption that community care was being provided which would improve the health status of the person. While there has been a huge shift in responsibility onto the community (which usually means the family), there has been no corresponding shift in the budget. Care in the community should not be seen as the cheap option.

Mental Health

The health strategy identifies several areas which are to be developed, including mental health. However, it is one of the least developed in the action plan. There is only one action identified:

> *Action 25: A New Action Programme for mental health will be developed and a national policy framework will be prepared by mid 2003.*

This is in contrast with what the WHO has shown in its research:

> *It was estimated that, in 1990, mental and neurological disorders accounted for 10 per cent of the total days lost due to all diseases and injuries. This was 12 per cent in 2000. By 2020, it is projected that the burden of these disorders will have increased to 15 per cent.*

> *The World Health Report 2001*
> *Mental Health: New Understanding, New Hope*

Access to Health Services

The Commission on Health Funding (1989) recommended that access to all necessary health services (to be determined on the basis of objective criteria) should be available by reference to individual need, rather than ability to pay or geographical location. This recommendation was adopted in the National Health Strategy. While equality of access now forms part of government policy, this is not the case in practice.

Research undertaken by the Combat Poverty Agency (2000) suggests that those with private health insurance have faster access to acute health services, and can afford to pay for the lifestyle changes necessary for good health, such as good diet or giving up smoking. It also shows that people living in rural areas face particular problems of access to the health services because of the difficulty and cost involved in travelling long distances to avail of health services. They also identify other less tangible barriers to health access, such as lack of access to appropriate health information, advice, support and preventative services. They point to the difficulties in accessing these services experienced by those with poor literacy skills. It was hoped that in the Budget of 2001 the Government would have raised the eligibility levels for medical cards, but this issue was not addressed. As a result, the eligibility level is lower than for some of the social welfare payments.

CORI welcomes the recognition that socio-economic and environmental factors are parts of the determinants of health. There is still a need to acquire relevant data to draw up and implement the plan to promote equality of health status among the disadvantaged groups in society.

National Anti-Poverty Strategy Review 2002
The NAPS Review 2002 set the following as key targets:
> To reduce the gap in premature mortality between the lowest and highest socio-economic groups by at least 10 per cent by 2007
> To reduce the gap in the low birth weight rates between children from the lowest and highest socio-economic group by 10 per cent from the current level, by 2007.
> The gap in life expectancy between the Traveller

> Community and the whole population will be reduced by at least 10 per cent by 2007.
> National guidelines will be put in place for the provision of respite care services to carers of older people and carers of disabled people by 2003.
> Access to orthopaedic services will be improved so that no on is waiting longer than 12 months for a hip replacement.

CORI Justice Commission welcomes the
> *"overall objective to reduce the inequalities that exist in the health of the population by making health and health inequalities central to public policy, by acting on the social factors influencing health, by improving access to health and personal social services for people who are poor or socially excluded, and by improving the information and research base in relation to health status and service access for these group".*

The targets set in this area are not as comprehensive as we would like. However there are more detailed targets expressed in the Framework Document. Some of these targets have been reiterated in the National Health Strategy, e.g. Health Impact Assessment will be carried out on all new Government policies by June 2002. This is very welcome but concern would have to be expressed that the framework document will only be put into place insofar as resources are available.

The Framework Document contains in detail the actions that are needed to ensure that the objective is fulfilled. It recognises that equity of access is a key factor to ensure social inclusion of those marginalised in society. Lack of access to services is a key concern also of those living in rural areas.

This is also recognised as a key factor in the National Health Strategy. However, the National Health Strategy is based on the two-tier system of healthcare that already exists which has contributed to inequity in the system. This we feel is a fundamental flaw of the strategy.

The Primary Care commitment of the National Health Strategy supports many of the actions given to achieve equity of access in the primary care services but it remains aspirational unless financial resources are put in place to ensure its delivery. This must be done in conjunction with local communities, in equal partnership with statutory bodies, meeting local needs.

Policy Proposals

- **Give far greater priority to community care and restructure the healthcare budget accordingly**

Overall, government should ensure that at least 35 per cent of the non-capital healthcare budget is allocated to community care. In the process, care should be taken to ensure that the increased allocation does not go to the GMS or the drug subsidy scheme.

- **Develop and implement targets on healthcare and health status within the National Anti-Poverty Strategy.**
- **Increase the percentage of the health budget allocated to the health promotion area.**
- **Subject labour-market policies to routine health impact study.**
- **Provide the childcare services with the additional resources necessary to implement the Child Care Act effectively.**
- **Implement the PPF 3.10.19 commitment to pilot community-based primary healthcare centres.**
- **Develop day-care centres for children (pre-school and crèche facilities).**
- **Develop nursing care of elderly people in their own community on the model of the hospice-care programme.**
- **Establish monitoring procedures which will ensure that the criteria for admission to continuing care for the elderly in receipt of state subvention for such services are administered in a manner that is flexible and sensitive to the needs of the population.**

- Provide respite care for elderly people and people with disabilities.
- Resource the implementation of the Task Force Report on the Travelling Community.
- Promote equality of access to services within the Irish healthcare system.
- Develop and resource mental health services, recognising that this will be a key factor in the health status of the population.
- Raise the eligibility level for the medical card.

We welcome the recognition in the health strategy of the need to develop information systems, and we look forward to the publication of the national information strategy.

The strategy is committed to the establishment of a Health Information Quality Authority. This is a very welcome development and, if the composition of the authority and the powers invested in it are sufficient to achieve its function, it has a large part to play in ensuring equity, quality standards and accountability.

The commitment to the monitoring and evaluation of the Health Strategy needs to be expanded and developed so that the consumer is an essential part of this process. Mechanisms need to be developed to represent the views of the health-service user at all levels in the decision-making process.

3.7 Education[2]

> **CORE POLICY OBJECTIVE: EDUCATION**
> To provide relevant education for all citizens throughout their lives, so that they can participate fully and meaningfully in developing themselves, their community and the wider society.

Arising out of its vision of society, CORI promotes an education system that is designed to enable people to establish right relationships with self, others, God and the environment. In particular, we promote an education system which:

- seeks to promote forms of equality which liberate those who are oppressed;
- recognises the dignity of every human person and values all human talents equally;
- adopts a holistic approach to the development of individuals so that every aspect of their personalities can grow in a balanced and harmonious way;
- balances individual achievement with co-responsibility and co-operation in service of the common good;
- encourages the capacity to analyse critically the norms and mores of the prevailing society, in order to challenge society's unjust structures;
- provides opportunities for people to participate fully in making decisions about their own education and that of their families.

CORI believes that education can be a powerful force in counteracting inequality and poverty, while recognising that, in many ways, the present education system has quite the opposite effect. Recent studies confirm the persistence of social class inequalities which are seemingly ingrained in the system (Clancy & Wall, 2000; McCoy, Doyle & Williams, 1999; Smyth, 1999; Whelan & Hannan, 1999). Even in the context of increased participation and economic boom, the education system

---

[2] *The Justice Commission acknowledges the work done by the CORI Education Commission in preparing this section.*

continues to mediate the vicious cycle of disadvantage and social exclusion between generations.

The inequalities in the education system are starkly portrayed in the under-representation of poorer socio-economic groups at third level (Clancy & Wall, 2000). However, this severe under-representation at third level is strongly linked to failures earlier in the education system, and to problems in the system as a whole. While there are a number of programmes and initiatives to tackle educational disadvantage, many of these initiatives simply involve providing additional resources for disadvantaged schools. This does not amount to positive discrimination, but simply results in a closing of the gap in terms of resources between schools in disadvantaged areas and others. Initiatives such as the 8-15 ESLI and the SSRI do adopt a more comprehensive and integrated approach to tackling disadvantage, but acting alone and in the absence of mainstreaming and wider systemic change, there are limits to what can be achieved through such initiatives.

CORI's policy in this area is based on a belief that early school leaving is a particularly serious manifestation of wider inequality in education, which is embedded in and caused by structures in the system itself. As such, inequalities in education can ultimately be tackled only by a sustained effort to address those features of the education system, as a whole, which help to create and sustain the problem of educational disadvantage. In this section, we will highlight four priority areas for education policy:

1. The need to make education spending less regressive across sectors and to target resources, within sectors, to individual schools, and within schools to children who are most affected by poverty.

2. The need to tackle the systemic features of the education system which contribute to inequality. The narrow academic focus of curriculum and assessment will be discussed in this regard.

3. The need to build on the White Paper and to provide the long-overdue resources necessary to develop comprehensively the provision of Adult and Community Education.

4. The need to address the problems of educational disadvantage within the context of an integrated area-based approach at the local level and greater co-ordination at the national level.

Funding on the Basis of Greatest Need

Under our present system of funding education, the state spends considerably less on the education of poor people than it does on the education of people from more comfortable backgrounds. For example, while the state spends about £21,242 on the education of someone who leaves school without a formal qualification, it spends over £50,526 on someone who completes a four-year programme at third level.[3] The great majority of the first group (early school-leavers) are from poor backgrounds, while 'graduates' are predominantly middle and upper class — hence the use of the term 'regressive' to describe the present system.

This regressive pattern of educational expenditure would appear to contravene the commitments to poverty-proofing contained in the National Anti-Poverty Strategy (NAPS). Such spending could be re-balanced through substantial targeted investment in pre-school and primary-school education, coupled with the provision of substantial resources for the development of second-chance Adult and Community Education. The targeting of resources, opportunities and supports to those who are disadvantaged is the clearest practical expression of the principles of equality and inclusiveness in education and in other areas of social policy. The government and the social partners have all committed to the targeting of investment in programmes designed to alleviate disadvantage and social exclusion. However, in the most recent 'targeted' initiative to tackle educational disadvantage at primary level — *Giving Children an Even Break by Tackling Disadvantage* (January 2001) —

---

3 *The estimates of expenditure provided here are derived from information obtained in Key Education Statistics 1988/89-1998/99 (Department of Education & Science).*

the investment has been spread so thinly that its capacity to impact on educational inequalities has been undermined.
In relation to the treatment of educational disadvantage within the NAPS, there is a clear and urgent need for the adoption of more focused targets. The current review of the NAPS offers an ideal opportunity to redress the weaknesses in the original strategy. Regrettably, only one of the educational aspirations of the NAPS (1997) was formulated in terms of a specific target. This target sought to '*reduce early school leaving such that the percentage of those completing the senior cycle will increase to at least 90% by the year 2000 and 98% by the year 2007*' (NAPS (1997), p. 9). However, recent surveys of school-leavers indicate that the overall completion rates at second level have lingered around the 81 per cent mark between 1993 and 1998. In relation to the treatment of educational disadvantage in schools, CORI has argued that priority should be given within the NAPS to early school-leavers who enter the labour market with no formal qualifications.[4] We believe that this prioritisation is justified on the basis that those without qualifications:

- experience significantly higher unemployment rates than other groups of school-leavers;
- have prospects, in employment terms, which are actually deteriorating while the prospects of others are improving;
- are drawn almost exclusively from poorer socio-economic groupings;
- have declined in numbers to a level where intensive intervention could be made for a relatively modest investment of resources.

For these reasons, CORI has supported the NESF (1997) view that an appropriate target to set is the complete elimination of early school-leaving (without a qualification), within a specified time frame. The National Anti-Poverty Strategy (1997) lost sight of the specific focus of the NESF when, although it stated a commitment to eliminate early school-leaving before the Junior Certificate, it set *no time-frame* for the achievement of this target. In prioritising the elimination of early

---

4 These include those who leave secondary school before the Junior Certificate and those who fail to obtain five passes in the Junior Certificate exam (see ESRI school leavers' surveys). Also included are those children who do not make the transition from primary school to secondary school, currently estimated at between 800 and 1,000 children each year (see Table 2.13 of DES Annual Statistical Reports).

school-leaving without a qualification, we do not want to neglect other aspects and manifestations of educational disadvantage. Thus we fully recognise the need, for example, to reduce the flow of disadvantaged young people from schools *after* the Junior Certificate, and to increase participation rates at third level by young people from disadvantaged backgrounds. However, for the reasons outlined, we think it is important to recognise the increasingly serious consequences, for individuals and for society, of leaving school without a formal qualification. In any event, many (although, by no means, all) of the policy measures designed to prevent early school-leaving without a qualification can also serve other objectives (e.g. senior cycle completion, third-level participation, etc.).

Tackling Systemic Factors in Schooling

While CORI supports special schemes and alternative programmes, we believe that there is a need to focus on the extent to which the system as a whole contributes to educational disadvantage. An approach that focuses on the system as a whole would alter fundamentally the experience of schooling, not just for those students who are disadvantaged, but for all students. Curriculum and assessment are among the main determinants of a student's experience of schooling. We have consistently been very critical of the narrow academic focus of curriculum and the limited use of different modes of assessment at second level.[5] Hence, we endorse the NCCA proposals for a revised curriculum and assessment in the Junior Certificate for all pupils (NCCA, 1999).

We believe that, from the perspective of all students, the established Leaving Certificate programme, especially its procedures for assessment and certification, is in need of reform. Alternative senior-cycle programmes such as the LCA tend to be practically oriented and focus on preparing young people for work and for life. Over recent years, this programme, together with the LCVP, have pioneered significant curricular and pedagogical innovation which should be mainstreamed

---

5 *For a fuller discussion of these issues, see CORI Education Commission (1998), Inequality in Education: The Role of Assessment and Certification. Analysis and Options for Change and CORI Education Commission (1998), The Points System - An Analysis and Review of Some Alternatives.*

across the system. Therefore, the Department of Education and Science should ask the NCCA to draw up a plan to ensure that innovations developed, within the LCA and LCVP, are incorporated in the established Leaving Certificate. CORI believes that it is necessary to move quickly to a unified senior-cycle programme that would offer several broad areas of study (academic, vocational, personal and social development, etc.). A single umbrella certificate relating to each of these areas is necessary.

Ultimately, the Leaving Certificate examination will need to recognise and certify a much wider range of human qualities. We have called for the immediate implementation of proposals in the report of the Commission on the Points System (1999) relating to 'radical and creative' ways of reforming assessment within the Leaving Certificate examination. Wide-ranging changes in senior-cycle assessment, especially if they were to include some school-based assessment, would mitigate many of the damaging effects of the points system. Further progress towards eliminating these damaging effects will require the creation of alternative pathways to third-level education and the provision of additional supports to students from disadvantaged backgrounds.

Adult and Community Education

Adult and community education have enormous potential as strategies for tackling social inequality and for developing citizenship and social solidarity. Adult education can represent a second chance for those adults who have not benefited from their schooling, and community education can be a very powerful strategy in addressing the underlying causes of poverty and educational disadvantage. CORI welcomes the publication of *Learning for Life: White Paper on Adult Education* (DES, 2000), which has signalled the long-overdue recognition of an area that has been almost completely neglected in terms of social policy up until now. As a policy document, the main strengths of the White Paper include the emphasis on strong principles and the fact that it contains a wide range of progressive and far-reaching proposals on the development of a framework for adult and community education. However, the implementation of the proposals and recommendations contained in the White Paper has been severely constrained by the limited increase in funding.

Despite the failure of the budget and the public-expenditure estimates to provide meaningful information on the funding of adult and community education, it would appear that expenditure increased by 18 per cent (£10.8m) following last year's budget. This was an extremely minor increase, considering the history of severe under-funding in this area. On reading the White Paper, one would have expected that the allocation of educational funding would have been dominated by large-scale increases in funding for adult and community education, *'the last area of mass education to be developed in Ireland'* (DES, 2000, p.200). However, that budget did not even release to the area of adult and community education the expected proportion of money already committed under the National Development Plan (see CORI, 2001).

In addition to the shortage of funding, the fragmented nature of emerging developments is a cause of serious concern. It is very difficult to understand the Government's failure over the past year to establish the National Adult Learning Council (NALC). The pivotal role of the NALC cannot be overstated given that its terms of reference include responsibility for co-ordination, policy-advice and the identification of priorities. The NALC and the Local Adult Learning Boards (LALBs) also serve to provide representation for the range of educational partners and for the community/voluntary sector, thereby ensuring the support and participation of a wide variety of interests in the development and implementation of adult and community education. In the absence of the NALC and the LALBs, there is a real danger that implementation will continue in an ad-hoc and fragmented manner. The NALC should be established without any further delay, in order to ensure participation and accountability in the implementation of the many positive recommendations contained in the White Paper.

In the interest of coherence and integration, it would also be beneficial to situate the implementation of the White Paper in the context of the implementation of broader social-inclusion strategies such as the National Anti-Poverty Strategy (NAPS). The NAPS explicitly acknowledges the relationship between education and poverty, and recognises the crucial role of life-long education and training in tackling poverty and social exclusion. However, it is regrettable that there are no specific targets to strengthen the support that is promised in the Strategy for lifelong learning, second-chance education and community-based education and training (Combat Poverty Agency, 2000, p. 60). The creation of such specific targets within the NAPS would strengthen the Government's resolve to implement the framework for adult and community education outlined in the White Paper.

Development of Integrated Strategies

CORI believes that the link between education and poverty can best be addressed within the context of an integrated area-based approach at the local level, and greater co-ordination between government departments at the national level. The recognition of the limitations of traditional forms of service delivery has been accompanied by a growing understanding of the complexity of our most persistent and entrenched social problems. Indeed, the multi-faceted and cumulative nature of educational disadvantage and social exclusion is among the strongest and most compelling justification for integration. The many dimensions of social exclusion can be seen in the relationships between education and poverty, in the links between ill health and poverty, and in the range of other social needs associated with poverty (CORI, forthcoming). A central goal of integrated strategies is to empower and build up the capacities of disadvantaged individuals, families and communities through participation.

The current legislative understanding of the term 'educational disadvantage' defines it as *the impediments to education arising from social or economic disadvantage which prevent students from deriving appropriate benefit from education in schools* (Education Act, 1998: 32/9). Given the multi-faceted and often cumulative nature of educational disadvantage and social exclusion, many of the impediments which prevent students from benefiting appropriately from education relate to areas of life well beyond the remit of the Department of Education and Science. Indeed, any policy to promote equality in educational outcomes between social classes can succeed only if accompanied by economic policies aimed at eliminating the income and wealth differentials which perpetuate educational inequality in the first place (Lynch, 1999: 173). Therefore, public policies aimed at the alleviation of disadvantage, if they are to be effective, will invariably have to incorporate substantial collaboration between a wide range of agencies and departments.

The principle of integration has been repeatedly endorsed by numerous government departments and in almost all recent government policy documents relating to the areas of education, health, justice, and welfare. Much progress has been made in developing models for the integrated delivery of services through case studies in the international literature. In addition, there is evidence that much good work has occurred at ground level here in Ireland through informal collaboration and pilot projects. However, the strong message which is emerging from experiences here in Ireland and internationally is that the organisation of integrated area-based strategies is constrained in the absence of collaboration at higher levels; it is also constrained by the failure to mainstream innovations which emerge through pilot projects. Collaboration on the ground must be mirrored by administrative and strategic collaboration at the highest levels.

The achievement of internal coherence within individual government departments is an essential pre-requisite of the wider inter-departmental integration that is necessary. Within the Department of Education and Science, the Committee on Educational Disadvantage will be ideally placed to enhance and promote integration between the different programmes and the various sections, on issues relating to educational disadvantage. This Committee must be *fully* established without further delay and provided with the resources necessary to fulfil its brief.

Ultimately, the development of integrated services can lead to a more holistic approach to the multi-dimensional problem of educational disadvantage. However, while there is some evidence of progress in relation to many aspects of the integrated approach, there is little evidence of the kind of commitment to systemic change that is essential to the achievement of integration. In truth, we are not convinced that the issue of systemic change is being taken seriously enough in relation to educational disadvantage and social exclusion more generally.

National Anti-Poverty Strategy Review 2002
The NAPS Review 2002 set the following as key targets:
> **To halve the proportion of pupils with serious literacy difficulties by 2006.**
> **To reduce the proportion of the population aged 16-64 with restricted literacy to below 10 to 20 per cent by 2007 (restricted literacy being defined as falling below 200-225 on the IALS scale or equivalent)**
> **To reduce the number of young people who leave the school system early, so that the percentage of those who complete upper second level or equivalent will reach 85 per cent by 2003 and 90 per cent by 2006.**

CORI Justice Commission are disappointed that the target to reduce early school leaving has been revised downward (from 98 per cent to 90 percent). However, we welcome the objective that:
> *to ensure that all young people leave the educational system with an adequate education and related qualification to support their full participation in the economy, in employment and in society. In addition all those who have already left school must have the opportunity to address any lack of educational experience and related qualifications that militates against their ability to participate fully in the economy, in employment and in society.*

Overall, we are concerned that these targets are not sufficiently precise. For example it is possible to reach the target of retaining 90 per cent of young people in upper second level by 2007 without impacting on the numbers leaving without qualification. There are vast differences between the opportunities available to a young person who drops out of school at 12 years as against one who leaves at 16 years with a good junior certificate qualification. More precise targets and measures of outcomes are needed to address this problem. The strategy accepts that 10% of young people will leave before completion of upper second level. The barriers that lead to this drop out need to be addressed.

Policy Proposals

- Complete the establishment of the Committee on Educational Disadvantage without further delay and provide it with the resources necessary to fulfil its brief especially in relation to:

    (a) The integration, co-ordination and mainstreaming of existing programmes and schemes within the Department of Education and Science, which aim to address educational disadvantage;

    (b) The dissemination of best practice in schools and the promotion of innovation in tackling educational disadvantage;

    (c) 'Disadvantage proofing' of policies and the identification of systemic factors which contribute to educational disadvantage.

- The Government should make an explicit commitment to eliminate early school-leaving (without a qualification) *within a specific time-frame* and the resources necessary to achieve this target should be made available through the budget.
- Increase the proportion of educational expenditure that is allocated to the primary sector and to pre-school education as a way of partially addressing the regressive nature of educational funding.

- Begin to implement the main recommendations of the Steering Group on the funding of Second Level Schools, especially those relating to disadvantage and equalising the funding of different types of schools.
- Increase the allocation of funds to the NCCA to enable it to:

    (a) Expedite reform of assessment at Junior Certificate level;
    (b) Provide for the commencement of change at senior cycle;
    (c) Incorporate innovative practice from LCA and LCVP into the Leaving Certificate Examination;
    (d) Move towards the creation of a unified senior-cycle programme, which would offer several broad areas of study (e.g., academic, vocational, personal and social development etc.)

- Radically increase the funding of Adult and Community Education to facilitate the implementation of priorities identified in the White Paper.
- Establish the National Adult Learning Council and the Local Adult Learning Boards immediately.
- Support the establishment of local partnerships, involving all the schools and other agencies in an area in the preparation of a plan for approval by the proposed Local Adult Learning Boards.
- Recognise second-chance education as an entitlement, and promote it to those who have been prioritised under current government policy as set out in the *White Paper on Adult Education*.
- Target an agreed significant proportion of state investment in work-based education and training to the least well qualified members of the labour force.
- Begin to address the education and training needs of people who are not paid a wage for their work (e.g., carers, women in the home, etc.)

- Revise the format of the public-expenditure estimate and budget statement for Education and Science to include a separate 'head' with detailed 'subheads' for Adult and Community Education.
- Provide significant resources to enable the National Children's Strategy to develop a multi-agency and multi-level integrated approach to combating disadvantage and social exclusion.
- Examine the current system of allocating public expenditure in the annual budget in order to assess the extent to which it maximises the participation of all relevant partners and facilitates the long-term sustainability of cross-departmental integrated initiatives.
- Develop agreed education and training programmes and resources on integration for policy-makers and service-providers.
- Provide disadvantaged young people with opportunities to influence educational policy and practice.
- Establish a right to lifelong education and training for people with physical and mental disabilities.
- Proceed with the full implementation of the Education recommendations of the *Report of the Task Force on the Traveller Community*.

3.8 Culture and Cultural Respect

> **CORE POLICY OBJECTIVE:**
> **CULTURE AND CULTURAL RESPECT**
> To ensure that all people can contribute to developing the underpinning values and meaning of society and can have their own cultures respected in this process, and to ensure that Ireland is open to welcoming people from different cultures and traditions in a way that is consistent with our history, our obligations as world citizens and with our current economic status

Culture and cultural respect constitute an important right of people within every society. Culture is defined by UNESCO as *'the whole complex of distinctive spiritual, material, intellectual and emotional features that characterise a society or social group. It includes not only the arts and letters, but also modes of life, the fundamental rights of the human being, value systems, traditions and beliefs.'*

Many people in Ireland today — particularly Travellers, immigrants, refugees, and asylum-seekers, among others — do not experience a society where the majority population respects their cultures. In fact, as we become more racially diverse, it becomes evident that Irish society is as capable of being as racist as any of our European neighbours who live in mixed racial societies.

Worldwide there has been a marked increase in the number of refugees forced to flee from their own countries in order to escape war, persecution, abuses of human rights, etc. Irish people have a long tradition of solidarity with peoples facing oppression within their own countries, but that tradition is not reflected in our policies towards refugees and asylum-seekers. Ireland should use its position in international forums, especially the UN Security Council, to highlight the causes of the displacement of peoples. In particular, Ireland should use these forums to challenge the production, sale and free access to arms and the implements of torture.

The number of asylum-seekers has increased from 3,883 in 1997 to 7,724 in 1999, and to 10,325 in 2001 (Department of Justice, Equality and Law Reform: 2001). The Government has responded to this increase in numbers by amending the 1996 Refugee Act and creating two independent statutory offices for the processing of asylum applications: the Refugee Applications Commissioner and the Refugee Appeals Tribunal. Additional staff and resources have been allocated to speed up the processing times for asylum applications. The Refugee Legal Service has also been given more staff and resources.

While asylum-seekers are assigned initial accommodation in Dublin, most are subsequently allocated accommodation at locations outside Dublin, pending completion of the asylum-seeking process. The Reception and Integration Agency has been established to perform this task. At the end of 2001, there were seventy-eight accommodations centres accommodating 4,246 asylum-seekers.

Government has also introduced a policy of 'direct provision', through which asylum-seekers receive accommodation and basic board, together with €19.05 (£15) per week per adult and €9.53 (£7.50) per child. Clearly, this is a completely inadequate amount of money and should be increased immediately to at least €45 (£35.44) a week for an adult and € 22.50 (£17.72) for a child.

Asylum-seekers are not the only foreigners who have come to Ireland in substantial numbers over recent years. Many Irish companies have also recruited staff from abroad. Without this increased number of skilled workers from outside Ireland, our economy would not have sustained its high growth rates. Yet government has been very slow to develop a cohesive, comprehensive policy to ensure that the new diversity of cultures and ethnic minorities within Ireland is respected as an enrichment of our society. Such an approach would recognise the need to integrate immigration policy with refugee and asylum-seeking policy. It would also require a recognition and acceptance of the importance of equality of respect and esteem in this area.

Ireland has both a moral and legal responsibility towards refugees and asylum-seekers. As a nation whose own people have themselves experienced the pain of emigration in the past, we should be to the forefront in implementing our obligations under the 1951 UN Geneva Convention relating to the Status of Refugees. The PPF states that *'policy on providing for asylum seekers' needs will be developed in consultation with Government Departments, State Agencies, NGOs and social partners'*. Government has been very slow in developing this consultation process. The Refugee Advisory Board, also committed to in the PPF, should by now have been established with substantial representation of refugee interest groups. The Non-Governmental Organisations (NGOs), already playing a major role in addressing the many issues that arise in this context, should be resourced to continue and develop their work.

Refugees and asylum-seekers, along with immigrant workers and returned emigrants, have the capacity to help cope with the skills shortages currently being experienced in the Irish economy, and thus should be regarded in a positive rather than a negative light. Consequently, we propose that asylum-seekers who currently are not entitled to take up employment should be allowed to do so with immediate effect. Removing this restriction would have a major impact on reducing their poverty and exclusion. In this context we regret the ending of the FAS asylum seekers project with no replacement giving entry to the labour market.

Government policy should encourage the creation of a multi-racial, inclusive society. One positive step in this area would be for government to implement the UN Convention on the Elimination of All Forms of Racial Discrimination (CERD).

Despite the fact that we have focused principally on the problems facing refugees and asylum-seekers, it is important to recognise that other groups, such as Travellers, also require their culture to be respected as of right. Implementation of the Report of the Task Force on the Travelling People has commenced, with the establishment of the structures recommended by the report. However, it is now very important to ensure that the recommendations of the report are fully implemented.

Policy Proposals

- Develop and resource a cultural policy which involves a dynamic conserving of traditions and beliefs, while also developing a vision for the future which incorporates hope, confidence and involvement.
- Use our position on the UN Security Council to curtail the production and sale of arms and instruments of torture and to eliminate child soilders.
- Establish the Refugee Advisory Board with substantial representation from refugee and asylum seekers interest groups.
- Recognise the right to work of all asylum-seekers whose application for asylum is at least six months old (and who are now entitled to take up employment).
- Provide fully resourced language training for asylum seekers.
- Put resources into processing the backlog of asylum applications.
- Give special consideration to gender and cultural sensitivities of asylum-seekers.
- Ensure proper protection and care of minors, while safeguarding their rights and the integrity of the asylum process.
- Give to asylum-seekers on 'direct provision', who are more than six months awaiting the processing of their

application, equal rights to accommodation and other social welfare provision, in line with the rights enjoyed by other Irish residents.
- Immediately increase the weekly allowance allocated to asylum-seekers on 'direct provision' to at least €45 (£35.44) a week for an adult and €22.50 (£17.72) for a child.
- Put sufficient resources into the Refugee Legal Service to ensure the provision is available on a daily basis at all centres where asylum-seekers are located.
- Ensure that the asylum process treats all nationalities and ethnic groups with fairness and equality.
- Ensure that the proposed carrier sanctions will not further jeopardise the health and safety of people wishing to seek asylum in Ireland.
- Increase financial supports for voluntary organisations which care for refugees and asylum-seekers. In particular, increase and secure the funding for the Irish Refugee Council.
- Provide special labour-market integration measures that address the special needs of refugees.
- Implement fully the recommendation of the Task Force Report on the Travelling People.

3.9 Participation

> **CORE POLICY OBJECTIVE: PARTICIPATION**
> To ensure that all people have a genuine voice in shaping the decisions that affect them and to ensure that all people can contribute to the development of society

The changing nature of democracy has raised many questions for policy-makers and others concerned about the issue of participation. Decisions often appear to be made without any real involvement of many affected by the decisions' outcomes. Voter apathy is widespread. Transparent accountability is demanded but rarely delivered. Recent polls confirm that people, especially young people, have little confidence in the political process. They are disillusioned because the political process fails to involve them in any real way, while also failing to address many of their core concerns. A new approach is clearly needed to address this issue.

An agreed foundation for argument on issues on which people disagree is a need that is becoming more obvious as political and mass communication systems develop. Most people are not involved in the processes that produce plans and decisions which affect their lives. They know that they are being presented with a *fait accompli*. More critically, they realise that they and their families will be forced to live with the consequences of the decisions taken. A lack of structures and systems to involve people in the decision-making process results in the exclusion and alienation of large sections of society. It causes and maintains inequality.

Any exclusion of people from debate on the issues that affect them is suspect. Such exclusion leaves those responsible for it open to charges concerning the arbitrary use of power. Some of the decision-making structures of our society and of our world allow people to be represented in the decision-making process. However, almost all of these structures fail to provide genuine participation for most people affected by their decisions. Our society and the world in which we live need decision-making structures that enable participation.

Real participation by all is essential if society is to develop and, in practice, to maintain principles guaranteeing satisfaction of basic needs, respect for others as equals, economic equality, and religious, social, sexual and ethnic equality.

Modern means of communication and information make it relatively easy to involve people in dialogue and decision-making. It is a question of political will — will the groups who have the power share it with others?

Some progress has been made in recent years. National programmes have a major impact on most people's lives. While these have produced negotiated pay agreements, they have also taken a range of decisions concerning other issues. The process which produced the most recent of these programmes, *Partnership 2000* and the *Programme for Prosperity and Fairness*, involved more groups than the previous three programmes. In particular, groups from the voluntary and community sector were invited by government to participate. This was a welcome initiative and much appreciated by the groups concerned.

A Forum for Dialogue on Civil Society Issues

More, however, is required. An issue that is contributing to disillusionment with the political process concerns the range of civil society issues that are of major concern to large numbers of people. These are issues that many people feel are not being addressed adequately; insofar as a discussion or debate does take place, they feel that they are not allowed to participate in any real way.

Social partnership, as we have pointed out, is one process aimed at improving the participation of various sectors in Ireland. However, it is in danger of being overloaded. The various social partners in the four pillars of social partnership — employers, trades unions, farmers and the community and voluntary sector — represent large segments of Irish society. However, they do not represent, nor do they claim to represent, all of Irish society. In fact, the case is made, with some legitimacy, that none of these social partners represents their own entire sector.

The development of a new forum within which a civil society debate could be conducted on an on-going basis would be a welcome addition to the political landscape in Ireland. Such a forum could make a major contribution to improving participation by a wide range of groups in Irish society.

Establishment of such a forum would ensure that civil society issues were not being loaded onto the already extensive work of social partnership in the socio-economic area. It would also be complementary to the work of the National Economic and Social Forum (NESF) and the National Economic and Social Council (NESC), both of which already have extensive agendas.

CORI proposes that government authorise and resource an initiative to identify how a civil society debate could be developed and maintained in an ongoing way in Ireland, and to examine how it might connect to the growing debate at European level around civil society issues.

There are many issues such a forum could address. One such issue that comes to mind, given recent developments in Ireland, is the issue of citizenship, its rights, responsibilities, possibilities and limitations in the twenty-first century. Another topical issue is the shape of the social model Ireland wishes to develop in the decades ahead. Do we follow a European model or an American one? Or do we want to create an alternative — and, if so, what shape would it have and how could it be delivered? The issues a civil society forum could address are many and varied. Ireland would benefit immensely from having such a forum.

Impact on the Democratic Process

Would a civil society forum and a new social contract against exclusion take from the democratic process? Democracy means 'rule by the people'. This implies that people participate in shaping the decisions that affect them most closely. What we have, in practice, is a highly centralised government in which we are 'represented' by professional politicians. The more powerful a political party becomes, the more distant it seems to become from the electorate. Party policies on a range of major issues are often difficult to discern. Backbenchers have little control over, or influence on, government ministers, opposition spokespersons or shadow cabinets. Even within the cabinet, some ministers seem to be able to ignore their cabinet colleagues.

The democratic process has certainly benefited from the participation of various sectors in other arenas such as social partnership. It would also benefit from taking up the proposals to develop a new social contract against exclusion and a new forum for dialogue on civil society issues.

The decline in participation is exacerbated by the primacy given to the market by so many analysts, commentators, policy-makers and politicians. Many people feel that their views or comments are ignored or patronised, while the views of those who see the market as solving most, if not all, of society's problems are treated with the greatest respect.

Markets have a major role to play. But it needs to be honestly acknowledged that markets produce very mixed results when left to their own devices. In terms of many policy goals, they are extremely limited. Consequently, other mechanisms are required to ensure that some re-balancing, at least, is achieved. The mechanisms proposed here are simply two that would be positive in improving participation in a twenty-first century society.

Policy Proposals

- Establish and resource a forum for dialogue on civil society issues. This initiative should identify how a civil society debate could be developed and maintained in an ongoing way in Ireland and should examine how it might connect to the growing debate at European level around civil society issues.
- Ensure that the County/City Development Board (CDB) structures are implemented as intended, and that participation is strengthened as they develop their city/county strategies.
- Ensure that Strategic Policy Committees (SPC) strengthen participation at local level.
- Resource the ongoing participation of the community and voluntary sector in both the CDB and SPC structures.
- Ensure that there is real and effective monitoring of policy implementation. Involve a wide range of perspectives in this process, thus ensuring inclusion of the experience of those currently excluded.
- Resource the participation in national social partnership of social partners within the community and voluntary sector.
- Act on the PPF commitment to resource voter education programmes for young people and socially excluded people.
- Government should investigate methods by which electoral participation can be increased.
- To assist the achievement of higher voter turnout, a commitment should be given to holding all elections and referenda on a Saturday, with polls open from 7 a.m. and 10p.m.

3.10 Promoting Sustainability

> **CORE POLICY OBJECTIVE:
> PROMOTING SUSTAINABILITY**
> To ensure that all development is socially, economically and environmentally sustainable

The search for a humane, sustainable model of development has gained momentum in recent times. After years of people believing that markets and market forces would produce a better life for everyone, major problems and unintended side effects have raised questions and doubts. There is a growing awareness that sustainability must be a constant factor in all development, whether social, economic or environmental.

Sustainable development has been defined in many different ways. Perhaps the best known definition is that contained in *Our Common Future* (World Commission on Environment and Development: 43):
development that meets the needs of the present without compromising the ability of future generations to meet their own needs.

Conventional economic models of development or progress fail to meet the needs of millions and millions of people on this planet today. This failure is evident even within better-off countries such as Ireland. These conventional economic models also compromise the ability of future generations to meet their needs. As this becomes more evident, there is a growing demand worldwide to find new models that will conserve the planet and its resources and empower people to meet their own needs and the needs of others.

Central to any model of development which has sustainability at its core must be a realisation of the need to move away from money-measured growth as the principal economic target and measure of success, and towards sustainability in terms of real-life social, environmental and economic variables. Already, within mainstream decision-making, this realisation has begun to have some impact. This can be seen, for example, in the growing awareness that environmental taxation should be recognised as a key policy instrument in dealing with environmental concerns. Public concern in the area of genetically modified food stands as another example. In the context of income and social welfare policy, the recent work on basic income undertaken under Partnership 2000 is a further example of the same search for policies that will be sustainable into the future. The growing demand for the recognition of unpaid work being done in society is yet another example. As can be seen from these examples, however, there is a long way to go before Ireland or the EU can claim to have placed sustainability at the centre of their development models.

A central initiative in this context should be the development of 'satellite' or 'shadow' national accounts. Our present national accounts miss fundamentals such as environmental sustainability. Their emphasis is on GNP/GDP as scorecards of wealth and progress. These measures, which came into widespread use during World War II, more or less ignore the environment, and completely ignore unpaid work. Only money transactions are tracked. Ironically, while environmental depletion is ignored, the environmental costs of dealing with the effects of economic growth, such as cleaning up pollution or coping with the felling of rain forests, are added to, rather than subtracted from, GNP/GDP. New scorecards are needed.

Already a number of alternative scorecards exist, such as the United Nations' Human Development Index (HDI), former World Bank economist Herman Daly's Index of Sustainable Economic Welfare (ISEW) and Hazel Henderson's Country Futures Index (CFI). In the environmental context, it is crucial that dominant economic models be challenged on (among other things) their assumptions that nature's capital (clean air, water and environment) are essentially free and inexhaustible; that scarce resources can always be substituted; and that the planet can continue absorbing human and industrial wastes which most economists tend to downplay as externalities.

Some governments have picked up on these issues, especially in the environmental area. They have begun to develop 'satellite' or 'shadow' national accounts, which include items not traditionally measured. Similar accounts should be developed for Ireland.

For the first time the issues of sustainability and environment have been addressed in a national partnership agreement. The Programme for Prosperity and Fairness (PPF) includes a commitment to ensure that:
> *the achievement of improvement in living standards in the shorter term is consistent with the long-term sustainability of economic and social progress, including protection of the environment.*

To facilitate this commitment, the NESC has engaged in a process to develop a framework of national progress indicators that measure economic, social and environmental development. These will include the value of unpaid work and the cost of environmental damage and resource consumption.

The PPF also includes actions on:
- a national greenhouse gas abatement strategy;
- a waste-management strategy;
- a strategy on genetically modified organisms;
- a strategy on water quality;
- a litter strategy;
- a strategy on eco-auditing.

These commitments do not constitute a comprehensive programme for sustainable development, but they are a step in the right direction. A comprehensive sustainable development programme would begin from the recognition that existing public policies in areas such as agriculture and transport specifically, but in most other areas as well, give powerful encouragement to unsustainable development. Policy-makers may be fearful of facing up to this situation, but it need not be a negative development.

For example, changes in framework policies for taxation and expenditure can encourage movement towards sustainability in many departmental policy fields such as farming and food, travel and transport, energy, patterns of work and more self-reliant local development, to name just a few.

Principles to Underpin Sustainable Development

Principles to underpin sustainable development have been suggested in a report for the European Commission, prepared by James Robertson in May 1997. Entitled *The New Economics of Sustainable Development*, the report argues that these principles would include the following:

- Systematic empowerment of people (as opposed to making and keeping them dependent) as the basis for people-centred development;
- Systematic conservation of resources and environment as the basis for environmentally sustainable development;
- Evolution from a 'wealth of nations' model of economic life to a 'one-world' economic system;
- Evolution from today's international economy to an ecologically sustainable, decentralising, multi-level one-world economic system;
- Restoration of political and ethical factors to a central place in economic life and thought;
- Respect for qualitative values, not just quantitative values;
- Respect for feminine values, not just masculine ones.

At first glance, these might not appear to be the concrete guidelines that policy-makers so often seek. Yet they are principles that are relevant to every area of economic life. They also apply to every level of life, ranging from personal and household to global issues. They impact on lifestyle choices and organisational goals. If these principles were applied to every area, level and feature of economic life, they would provide a comprehensive checklist for a systematic policy review.

It is also important that any programme for sustainable development should take a realistic view of human nature, recognising that people are altruistic and selfish, co-operative and competitive. Consequently, it is important to develop the economic system to reward activities that are socially and environmentally benign (and not the reverse, as at present). This, in turn, would make it easier for people and organisations to make choices that are socially and environmentally responsible.

One aspect of the environment that needs to be addressed is the issue of changing climate. Government, through its National Climate Change Strategy, is addressing this issue. This strategy proposed to impose (unspecified) taxes on oil, gas, coal and other fossil fuels to be phased in from 2002. However, while there have been some steps forward, incorporated into Budget 2002, few of these taxes have been implemented. The strategy also proposes (among other things):

- The conversion of the coal-fired power station at Moneypoint;
- Reductions in methane emissions from agriculture by reducing the national herd;
- The provision of an option for industry to participate in 'emissions trading' and voluntary agreements;
- Changes in the grant scheme for new-house purchases to promote energy efficiency;
- Changes in vehicle registration tax to favour more fuel-efficient transport.

The development of this strategy is most welcome and needs to be acted upon with increased urgency, as the issue of climate change is critical.

The following environmental issues are among other areas of concern at this time.

Waste Disposal

The recent emergence of a landfill shortage, alongside the continued discovery of illegal dumps, comes as no surprise. Ireland has, until recently paid scant attention to the issue of waste disposal. Much of what is dumped can be recycled, yet in the Republic of Ireland only 1 per cent of the 1.22 million tonnes of household waste is recycled annually. Similarly, industry recycles only 8 per cent of its waste. Contrast this with the potential 80 per cent of household waste and 94 per cent of industrial waste that is recyclable.

Industry in all sectors will have to use fewer material inputs and emit fewer wastes. To facilitate this, government needs to move towards making material inputs and waste disposal far more expensive, and towards making increasing demands for the durability, repairability and recyclability of goods. Examples of such government action can be seen in the USA (liability laws for the disposal of toxic materials) and in Germany (legislation compelling car manufacturers to take back vehicles for recycling at the end of their useful lives).

Households will also have to change their behaviour. Campaigns to encourage and facilitate recycling are necessary, while incentives to recycle rather than landfill need to be put in place.

Greenhouse Gas Emissions

Between 1990 and 1998, greenhouse gas emissions have been increasing rather than decreasing. These emissions now exceed the limits agreed under the Kyoto protocol. CORI Justice Commission welcomes Ireland's ongoing commitment to this protocol, despite the refusal of the USA to ratify its implementation. However, these emissions are a major cause of climate change, and it is in all our interests to ensure that the limits agreed in the Kyoto protocol are met. The Irish Government and the European Commission agreed a target of a 12 per cent reduction of CO_2 emissions by 2010. The full implementation of the aforementioned National Climate Change Strategy, and its associated new taxes, is necessary to achieve progress on this issue.

Energy
Energy must be used far more efficiently. Huge improvements in the efficiency of energy use are possible at little or no net cost. The obstacles to implementing these improvements are institutional (the structure of markets, the inertia of governments, the power of vested interests). The blockages to having sustainable energy policies are not economic or technological, but political.

The recent opening of the THORP reprocessing plant at Sellafield pushed the issue of nuclear energy higher up the agenda. Ironically, the Irish Government contributed to this plant by voting funding for it in the EU Budget. However, we welcome the legal initiatives taken to prevent the further operation of the plant. The Irish people have made it clear on many occasions that they wanted a nuclear-free country — this includes their air and seas. Clearly, this issue will not go away. Further strategies are necessary to have the activities of Sellafield reduced.

River-Water Quality
During the 1990s, the proportion of Ireland's rivers that were unpolluted fell from 72 per cent to 67 per cent. This is a worrying trend and needs initiatives to ensure it is reversed. It is clear that existing legislation to protect our inland watercourses from pollution is neither adequate nor effective.

Genetic Engineering (GE)
Genetic engineering refers to a set of technologies that artificially move genes across species boundaries to produce new organisms. The techniques involve the manipulation of genetic material and other biologically important chemicals. The resultant organisms have new combinations of genes, and therefore new combinations of traits that are not found in nature and, indeed, not possible through normal breeding techniques. Proponents of the technology, mainly multinational agribusiness corporations, argue that genetically engineered crops are necessary to feed a growing world population.

By contrast, opponents of agricultural biotechnology claim that genetic engineering will not feed the hungry people in our world. Only sustainable agriculture and equitable social and economic policies at local and global level can effectively tackle malnutrition, hunger and poverty.

Critics of genetic engineering maintain that it is hazardous to human health and the environment, and that it will undermine biodiversity. Given the risks to human health and the environment, and the complex ethical, economic and social issues involved, we believe that a moratorium should be placed on the deliberate release of genetically engineered organisms.

Policy Proposals

- **Sustainability-proof all public policy initiatives and provision.**
- **Develop 'satellite' national accounts that include the value of all unpaid work and the costs of all environmental damage and resource consumption.**
- **Restructure the tax system in favour of environmentally benign development and higher levels of employment and useful work.**
- **Terminate subsidies and other public-expenditure programmes that encourage unsustainable development.**
- **Introduce public purchasing policies that encourage contractors to adopt sustainable practices.**
- **Develop more self-reliant local economies.**
- **Develop indicators to measure economic, social and environmental performance and progress.**
- **Develop accounting, auditing and reporting procedures to establish the sustainability performance of businesses and other organisations.**
- **Introduce demand-reduction policies in areas such as energy and transport, and tackle the implications of such reduction.**

- Fully introduce the National Climate Change Strategy, including the introduction of new taxes on oil, gas, coal and other fossil fuels.

ON WASTE
- Develop a policy for resource management, and achieve waste-reduction targets by implementing relevant sections of the Waste Management Act, 1996.
- Provide households with incentives to recycle rather than landfill their waste.
- Allocate substantial resources to the development of recycling facilities.
- Set a target of recycling 40 per cent of household waste by 2010.

ON POLLUTION
- Put mechanisms in place to ensure that the targets of a 12 per cent CO_2 reduction by 2010, agreed by the Irish Government and the European Commission, are met.
- Continue to pursue strategies to achieve the reduction of activities at Sellafield.

ON WATER
- Review the Water Pollution Acts and increase the level of statutory fines with a scale from €6,348 (£5,000) to a maximum of €150,000 (£118,135).
- Implement a nutrient-management plan on a national basis as one effective measure to protect against agricultural pollution of watercourses.
- Review water-pricing policies and introduce a water charge, which is equitable and is levied on high-consumption water-users, to ensure conservation of our water supplies.

ON GENETIC ENGINEERING (GE)

- Introduce a five-year moratorium on the deliberate release of GE organisms. During this period:
  - Promote public debate about the desirability of genetic engineering and fund independent research into the health and environmental risks associated with GE;
  - Insist that there be segregation at the source of all genetically engineered organisms;
  - Reform the way the Environmental Protection Agency (EPA) deals with applications to release GE organisms into the environment.

- Facilitate a full-scale public debate on both the benefits and risks involved in GE, based on comprehensive scientific knowledge and a full airing of the economic, social and ethical implications of biotechnology.
- Fund appropriate research in parallel with such a consultative process.
- Introduce legislation that protects the consumer and the environment, rather than the interests of multinational corporations.

ON THE ENVIRONMENTAL PROTECTION AGENCY (EPA)

- Review the interface between the EPA and An Bord Pleanála to ensure that the environmental impact and sustainability of industrial developments are thoroughly assessed in an integrated way.

3.11 Rural Development

> **CORE POLICY OBJECTIVE:**
> **RURAL DEVELOPMENT**
> To secure the existence of substantial numbers of viable communities in all parts of rural Ireland where every person would have meaningful work, adequate income and social services, and where infrastructures needed for sustainable development would be in place

Rural Ireland continues to change dramatically. According to the most recent census, 46 per cent of Ireland's population live in small villages and in the open countryside. There is a decline in farm numbers, however. Those in farming now account for only one-quarter of the rural labour force, and are a minority of the rural population. Furthermore, fewer farm children seek a future in farming.

Among its many characteristics, rural Ireland has high dependency levels, increasing out-migration and many small farmers living on very low incomes. Only a minority of farmers are at present generating an adequate income from farming, and even on these farms, incomes lag considerably behind the national average. The National Farm Survey (2000) estimates that the average family farm income (excluding off-farm income) was €14,605 (£11,502) in 2000. It noted great variations in income depending on the size of the farm. Overall, full-time farmers had an average farm income of €27,506 (£21,663) and part-time farmers €6,241 (£4,915).

Off-farm income is extremely important among farm families, especially in the western region. The recent Household Budget Survey indicates that only 40.6 per cent of farm-household income came from farming, while the National Farm Survey shows that 45 per cent of farm households earn off-farm income. This situation is likely to intensify in the coming years, thus increasing the importance of additional off-farm income being available if rural poverty and social exclusion are to be addressed.

There have been increases in the numbers employed in rural Ireland over recent years, but in many cases these increases have lagged behind the pace of national increases.

The Census Atlas of Agriculture, *Irish Agriculture in Transition,* confirms the *'striking contrast between the west and north-west and the south and east in the use of land resources'*. It states that *'the boundary has been shifting southwards and the divergence between these two parts of the state has increased'*. It indicates that, by 2007, that there will be a core of commercial farms operating competitively in a market environment dominated by world farm-commodity prices, located mainly in the southwest. Smaller-scale producers on the fringes of these areas will be increasingly vulnerable to economic forces. A second tier of farmers will depend heavily on direct payments, legitimised on the basis that landholders provide 'public goods' especially by managing the environment or because their farms are in disadvantaged areas.

This kind of a shift in the patterns of Irish agriculture has, and will continue to have, real consequences for rural society generally. Long-term strategies to address the failures of current policies on critical issues such as infrastructure development, the national spatial imbalance, public transport and local involvement in core decision-making are urgently required. Recognition that current development policies are largely city-led is also necessary, and this approach needs to be re-balanced.

The 1999 White Paper on rural development is welcome in that it provides an outline of a vision to guide rural-development policy as we have advocated for over a decade. In so doing, it accepts that the statement of a vision is a necessary first step in moving forward. CORI Justice Commission also welcomes the identification by the White Paper of much that is already being done, under a variety of headings in all areas of rural development. However, there was little in terms of new and imaginative policies proposed for the implementation of the vision, and no commitment of new and measurable resources to attain the objectives set out.

The PPF sets out objectives for rural development, objectives we affirm. These state:
As set out in the White Paper, the objective of Government is to promote the economic and social development of rural communities in which there will be:

- *vibrant sustainable communities;*
- *sufficient income/employment opportunities to allow people to live in dignity;*
- *access to public services, including education, social and other services, housing, transport and infrastructure;*
- *participation in decision-making structures affecting them;*
- *maintenance of cultural identity;*
- *respect for the rural environment and sustainable development;*
- *protecting the environment and the preservation and enhancement of the culture and heritage of rural areas, including Gaeltacht areas*

(Framework II 2.5).

Clearly, the scale of the infrastructure and investment deficit in rural Ireland is unacceptably high. The recently launched CLAR programme will go a little way towards addressing this. However, far more is required if rural Ireland is to be viable in the twenty-first century.

Policy Proposals

- **'Decouple' all direct payments from production and introduce a direct payment in the form of a basic income for each person.**
- **Reappraise the concept of work. In doing this, the potential of the social economy should be incorporated, the range of activities of the Farm Relief Service broadened, and the facilitation of family-farm inheritance should be ensured.**

- Ensure the provision of basic infrastructure and services, based more on principles of equity and social justice, than on cost effectiveness, and take particular account of rural disadvantage.
- Ensure the provision of a reliable and appropriate transport system, by providing resources for the development of local-transport strategies and initiatives tailored to meet the needs of the local community.
- Reverse the trend of centralising services away from local communities in areas such as healthcare, education, post offices, etc.
- Locate rural housing in the countryside, restrict the current practice of concentrating dwellings in the largest towns, and thus contribute to the future well-being of rural villages.
- Structure housing lists to reflect rural needs. In particular, in rural areas, develop a framework to guide planning policy, which is focused on supporting and sustaining viable rural communities and protecting and enhancing the rural environment.
- Facilitate and advance authentic representation of rural citizens.
- Ensure that public-service bodies take steps to inaugurate an effective and ongoing consultative process with all rural citizens.
- Overhaul the model for development in agriculture to take effective account of the difficulties of smaller farmers.
- Reappraise programmes to create employment for part-time farmers with a view to targeting effectively the needs of smaller farmers.
- Support programmes to create employment for part-time farmers, with a view to targeting effectively the needs of smaller farmers.
- Develop policies, which encourage alternative farm enterprises through the promotion of quality (including organic) food production and processing.

- Support additional special outreach education programmes in rural areas, particularly those where no major third-level colleges are located.
- Promote research on initiatives that will develop information systems and technologies in a manner that will enhance, rather than detract from, the viability of rural communities.

3.12 Official Development Assistance

> **CORE POLICY OBJECTIVE:**
> **OFFICIAL DEVELOPMENT ASSISTANCE**
> To ensure that Ireland plays an active and effective part in promoting genuine development in the countries of the South (the Third World) and to ensure that all Ireland's policies are consistent with such development

Today, almost one-fifth of the world's population, 1.3 billion people, lives in absolute poverty on less than one dollar a day. This is a figure anticipated to increase to 1.7 billion people by 2015. In Africa alone, over 90 per cent of the population lives in abject poverty. The vast majority of those who experience this level of poverty live in the South (the Third World).

The totally unacceptable division between rich and poor is largely attributable to unfair trade practices and to the backlog of unpayable debt owed by the countries of the South to other governments, to the World Bank, the International Monetary Fund (IMF) and to commercial banks.

These levels of poverty have disastrous consequences for the populations of indebted countries. Governments that are obliged to dedicate large percentages of their country's GDP to debt repayments cannot afford to pay for health and educational programmes for their people. Over 800 million people do not get enough daily food and 500 million are chronically undernourished. In particular, child mortality rates are high.

Poor people spend between 50 and 80 per cent of their incomes on food and water. At present, 20 per cent of the world's population does not have enough water to meet its needs, and this figure is set to rise to 30 per cent by 2025. The total cost of providing this water is $70

Official Development Assisatnce

billion, as against an annual level of global military expenditure of $780 billion.

Poverty is a root cause of regional conflicts and civil wars. States and societies that are poor are prone to conflict. It is very difficult for governments to govern adequately when their people cannot afford to pay taxes, and industry and trade are almost non-existent. Poverty is also a major cause of environmental degradation. Large-scale food shortages, migration and conflicts lead to environmental pressures.

Clearly, poverty in the southern world threatens the very survival of all peoples. It is the major injustice in a world that is not, as a unit, poor. Now, more than ever, as Ireland becomes more prosperous, the Irish Government must exercise its voice within the European Union and in world institutions, to ensure that the elimination of poverty becomes the focus of all policy development.

CORI Justice Commission believe that Ireland's representatives at the World Bank and the IMF should be more critical of the policies adopted by these bodies. The Department of Finance annual report on Ireland's involvement in these organisations reveals an alarming degree of unconditional support. According to the Report, Ireland has supported the World Bank in all of the following areas: poverty reduction, gender issues, private-sector development, governance issues and corruption, military spending, post-conflict initiatives and environmentally sustainable projects. This level of support does not match Irish public opinion. NGOs, such as the Debt and Development Coalition, which have done much work on these issues, are very critical of the World Bank in its policies on issues such as poverty reduction, gender and the environment. We believe that this criticism of government is well founded.

On a positive note, we welcome the commitment by the Government to increase Ireland's Official Development Assistance for poor countries to the UN target of 0.7 per cent of GNP by 2007. Budget 2002 achieved the interim target of 0.45 per cent of GNP previously set, by allocating

€372m (£293m). Reaching the UN target by 2007 necessitates further increases in the years ahead. We strongly urge the next Government to adhere to this target and to make the necessary increases each year.

The recent UNAIDS report (2001) revealed that there are now 28.1 million Africans with HIV/AIDS. In 2000, there were 3.4 million new infections and 2.3 million deaths; 15,000 new infections are occurring daily. Kofi Annan, the UN Secretary-General, has described the epidemic as 'an unparalleled nightmare' whose health, social, economic and family consequences are far beyond any ever previously experienced. In the worst-suffering African countries, over 30 per cent of the adult population has HIV/AIDS. In the least infected countries around 7 per cent of the adult population has contracted the disease. To date, there is no cure for HIV/AIDS. The UN also notes that the number of people infected by this disease is increasing rapidly in other areas of the third and developing world, such as in China, India and other parts of Asia.

In Budget 2002, the Government allocated €34m (£26.7m) to HIV/AIDS programmes in poor countries. This is a welcome start and an action that should be matched by many more governments worldwide. However, given the scale of the crisis, further funding will be required. Ireland should also play a role in adopting a leadership position within European and international communities, to encourage other states to fund programmes and research aimed at resolving this growing crisis.

Policy Proposals

- Ensure that Irish government policy is consistent with policies on **Official Development Assistance**.
- Take a far more proactive stance at government level on ensuring that Irish and EU policies towards countries in the South are just.
- We strongly urge the next Government to adhere to the commitment to increase Official Development Assistance to the UN target of 0.7 per cent of GNP by 2007. Reaching

that target necessitates further increases in the years ahead.
- Support the international campaign for the liberation of the poorest nations from the burden of the backlog of unpayable debt.

In 1997, Third World debt totalled over $2.2 trillion. In the same year, nearly $250 billion was repaid in interest and loan principal. Africa alone spends four times more on interest on its loans than on healthcare. For every €1 given in aid by rich countries, poor countries pay back nearly €4 in debt repayments.

It is only through debt cancellation that the poorest countries will ever be to able to remove the burden of debt. An international campaign, supported in Ireland by the Jubilee 2000 campaign, sought to have this debt cancelled. It is not possible for these countries to develop the kind of healthy economies that would facilitate debt repayment, when millions of their people are being denied basic healthcare and education and are either unemployed or earn wages so low that they can barely survive. As we have said already, the Government's present position on this issue is untenable.

- Work for changes in the existing international trading régimes, to encourage fairer and sustainable forms of trade. In particular, resource the development of Ireland's policies in the WTO to ensure that this goal is pursued.
- Budget 2002 recognised, for the first time, the need to support Eastern Europe, as part of official development aid. These post-communist countries deserve this aid and additional allocations in the years to come.
- Take up a leadership position within European and international communities to encourage other states to fund programmes and research aimed at resolving the AIDS/HIV crisis.

4. VALUES

Today, many people ask questions such as: 'If Ireland of the Celtic Tiger is so good, why do we meet so many anxious faces on our streets?' 'Why are so many people experiencing stress in meeting their commitments, be they financial, social, family, etc?' 'Why do so many parents have a struggle to find the resources necessary to keep their children in school?' 'Why are so many people homeless or living in overcrowded accommodation?' 'Why is there so much fear and anxiety in our communities?' As the pace of change escalates, those who have the economic and social resources acquire the equipment necessary to ride the crest of the present boom, while a large minority lives in fear of being submerged. Those on the crest of the boom have anxieties about staying there. This anxiety fuels the tendency to accumulate more and more to the point where 'greed is good'. Meanwhile, those who struggle to 'hang on' are feeling their grip loosening, and the prospect of being part of this society becoming more remote.

This reflection brings to the fore the issue of values. Our fears are easier to admit than our values. Do we as a people accept a two-tier society in fact, while deriding it in principle? This dualism in our values allows us to continue with the status quo, which, in reality, means that it is okay to exclude between a quarter and a third of the population from the mainstream of life of the society, while substantial resources and opportunities are channelled towards other groups in society. This dualism operates at the levels of individual people, communities and sectors.

Christian Values
CORI's concerns in this area are deeply rooted in Christian values. Christianity subscribes to the values of both human dignity and the centrality of the community. The person is seen as growing and developing in a context that includes other people and the environment. Justice is understood in terms of relationships. The Christian scriptures understand justice as a harmony that comes from fidelity to right

relationships with God, people and the environment. **A just society is one that is structured in such a way as to promote these right relationships so that human rights are respected, human dignity is protected, human development is facilitated and the environment is respected and protected.**

As our societies have grown in sophistication, the need for appropriate structures has become more urgent. While the aspiration that everyone should enjoy the good life, and the good will to make it available to all, are essential ingredients in a just society, the good life will not happen without the deliberate establishment of structures to facilitate its development. In the past, charity, in the sense of alms-giving by some individuals on an arbitrary and ad hoc basis, was seen as sufficient to ensure that everyone could cross the threshold of human dignity. Calling on the work of social historians, it could be argued that charity in this sense was never an appropriate method for dealing with poverty. Certainly, it is not a suitable methodology for dealing with the problems of today. As recent world disasters have graphically shown, charity and the heroic efforts of voluntary agencies cannot solve these problems on a long-term basis. Appropriate structures should be established to ensure that every person has access to the resources needed to live life with dignity.

Few people would disagree that the resources of the planet are for the use of the people — not just the present generation, but also the generations still to come. In Old Testament times, these resources were closely tied to land and water. A complex system of laws about the Sabbatical and Jubilee years (Lev 25: 1–22, Deut 15: 1–18) was devised to ensure, on the one hand, that no person could be disinherited, and, on the other, that land and debts could not be accumulated or the land exploited.

These reflections raise questions about ownership. Obviously, there was an acceptance of private property, but it was not an exclusive ownership. It carried social responsibilities. We find similar thinking among the leaders of the Early Christian Community. St John Chrysostom, speaking to those who could manipulate the law so as to accumulate wealth to the detriment of others, taught that *'the rich are in the possession of the goods of the poor even if they have acquired them honestly or inherited them legally'* (Homily on Lazarus). These early leaders also established that a person in extreme necessity has the right to take from the riches of others what s/he needs, since private property has a social quality deriving from the law of the communal purpose of earthly goods (*Guadium et Spes* 69–71).

In more recent times, Pope Paul VI said *'private property does not constitute for anyone an absolute and unconditional right. No one is justified in keeping for his/her exclusive use what is not needed when others lack necessities.... The right to property must never be exercised to the detriment of the common good'* (*Populorum Progressio* No.23). Pope John Paul II has developed the understanding of ownership, especially in regard to the ownership of the means of production. One of the major contributors to the generation of wealth is technology. The technology we have today is the product of the work of many people through many generations. Through the laws of patenting and exploration, a very small group of people has claimed legal rights to a large portion of the world's wealth. Pope John Paul II questions the morality of these structures. He says *'if it is true that capital as the whole of the means of production is at the same time the product of the work of generations, it is equally true that capital is being unceasingly created through the work done with the help of all these means of production'*. Therefore, no one can claim exclusive rights over the means of production. Rather that right *'is subordinated to the right to common use, to the fact that goods are meant for everyone'*. (*Laborem Exercens* No 14). Since everyone has a right to a proportion of the goods of the country, society is faced with two responsibilities regarding economic resources: firstly, each person should have sufficient to access the good life; and secondly, since the earth's resources are finite, and since 'more' is not necessarily 'better', it is time that society faced the question of putting a limit on the wealth that any person or corporation can accumulate.

Interdependence, mutuality, solidarity and connectedness are words that are used loosely today to express a consciousness which is very Christian. All of creation is seen as a unit that is dynamic — each part is related to every other part, depends on it in some way, and can also affect it. When we focus on the human family, this means that each person depends on others initially for life itself, and subsequently for the resources and relationships needed to grow and develop. To ensure that the connectedness of the web of life is maintained, each person is meant to reach out to support others in ways that are appropriate for their growth and in harmony with the rest of creation. This thinking respects the integrity of the person, while recognising that the person can achieve his or her potential only in right relationships with others and the environment. All of this implies the need for appropriate structures and infrastructures.

6. CONCLUSION

In this socio-economic review CORI Justice Commission has presented its analysis of the present socio-economic situation in Ireland, paying special attention to the sectors that have not benefited mush in recent years. We proposed *An Agenda for Fairness* aimed at ensuring economic development, social equity and sustainability in the medium to long term. Within this agenda we proposed and outlined a wide range of policy initiatives that should form the basis of any movement towards building such a future. These initiatives should form part of all policy development in the years immediately ahead. Sufficient resources will exist in the next few years to fund these policy initiatives. All our proposals are made within responsible fiscal parameters.

We do not claim to have all the answers. However, we make our proposals as a contribution to the public debate on what the key priorities in the socio-economic arena should be in the years ahead. All responses are most welcome.

REFERENCES

Agenda 21 (1993), *The Earth Summit's Agenda for Change*, Michael Keating, Geneva: Centre for our Common Future.

Bacon and Associates (2000), *An Economic Evaluation of Trends and Prospect*, Dublin: Stationery Office.

Bacon and Associates (1998), *An Economic Assessment of Recent House Price Developments*, Dublin, Stationery Office.

Bacon, Peter (1998), *The Fiscal Treatment of Housing in Ireland: An Overview*, Foundation for Fiscal Studies Annual Conference.

Bacon, Peter (1999), *The Housing Market: An Economic Review and Assessment*, Dublin: Stationery Office.

Callan, T., B. Nolan, B. Whelan, C. Whelan and J. Williams (1996), *Poverty in the 1990s*, Dublin, Oak Tree Press.

Central Bank of Ireland (various), *Quarterly Bulletins*, Dublin.

Central Statistics Office (2001), *Household Budget Survey 1999–2000 Preliminary Report*, Dublin, Stationery Office.

Central Statistics Office (various), *Balance of International Payments*, Dublin, Stationery Office.

Central Statistics Office (various), *Consumer Price Index*, Dublin, Stationery Office.

Central Statistics Office (various), *Household Budget Survey*, Dublin, Stationery Office.

Central Statistics Office (various), *Industrial Earnings and Hours Worked*, Dublin, Stationery Office.

Central Statistics Office (various), *Labour Force Survey*, Dublin, Stationery Office.

Central Statistics Office (various), *Quarterly National Household Survey*, Dublin, Stationery Office.

Central Statistics Office (1995), *Population and Labour Force Projections: 1996–2026*, Dublin, Stationery Office

Clancy, P. (1995), *Access to College: Patterns of Continuity and Change,*. Dublin, Higher Education Authority.

Clark, C.M.A. and C. Kavanagh (1995), 'Basic Income and the Irish Worker' in Reynolds B. and S. Healy, *An Adequate Income Guarantee for All: Desirability, Viability, Impact*, Dublin, CORI.

Clark, C.M.A. and J. Healy (1997), *Pathways to a Basic Income*, Dublin, CORI.

Collins, M.L. and C. Kavanagh (1998), 'For Richer, For Poorer: The Changing Distribution of Household Income in Ireland, 1973–94', in Healy, S. and B. Reynolds, *Social Policy in Ireland: Principles, Practice and Problems,* Dublin, Oak Tree Press.

Commission on Health Funding (1989), Final Report, Dublin, The Stationery Office.

Commission on Social Welfare (1986), Final Report, Dublin, The Stationery Office.

Commission on the Points System (1999), *Final Report and Recommendations,* Dublin, The Stationery Office.

CORI Education Commission (1998), *Inequality in Education: The Role of Assessment and Certification — Analysis and Options for Change,*. Dublin, CORI Education Commission.

CORI Education Commission (1998), *The Points System — An Analysis and Review of Some Alternatives,* Dublin, CORI Education Commission.

CORI Education Commission (1999), *Social Transformation and Lifelong Learning,* Dublin, CORI Education Commission.

CORI Justice Commission (1998), *Priorities for Progress: Towards a Fairer Future,* Dublin, CORI.

Curran, E. (1998), 'Absolute Moral Norms in Christian Ethics', in *Christian Ethics: An Introduction*, Bernard Hoose, (Ed), London, Cassell.

Curtin, C., T. Haase and H. Tovey (1996), *Poverty in Rural Ireland: A Political Economy Perspective*, Dublin, Oak Tree Press.

References

Deloitte and Touche (September 1998), *Review of Community Employment Programme*, Dublin, Department of Enterprise, Trade and Employment.

Department of Agriculture and Food (28 January 1998), Press Release announcing White Paper on Rural Development.

Department of Agriculture, Food and Rural Development (2001), CLAR Programme on Rural Development, Dublin, Stationery Office.

Department of Education and Science (1999), *Key Educational Statistics 1987/88–1997/98,* Department of Education and Science.

Department of Education and Science (1999), *The New Deal. A plan for educational opportunity,*. Dublin, Government Publications.

Department of Education and Science (2000), *Learning for Life: White Paper on Adult Education,* Dublin, Government Publications.

Department of Enterprise, Trade and Employment (1998), *Employment Action Plan.*

Department of Finance (2001), *Budget 2002*, Dublin, Stationery Office.

Department of Finance (2002), *Monthly Economic Bulletin, January 2002*, Dublin, Stationery Office.

Department of Health (1994), *Shaping a Healthier Future: A Strategy for Effective Healthcare in the 1990's*, Dublin, Stationery Office.

Department of Health and Children (1998), *Working for health and well-being: strategy statement 1998–2001,* Dublin.

Department of Health and Children (2000), *National Health Promotion Strategy 2000–2005*.

Department of Justice, Equality and Law Reform (2001), *Annual Report 2001*, Dublin, Stationery Office.

Department of Social, Community and Family Affairs (various), *Statistical Information and Social Welfare Services*, Dublin, Stationery Office.

Department of Social, Community and Family Affairs (2002), Building an Inclusive Society, Dublin, Stationery Office.

Department of Social, Community and Family Affairs (2002), Framework Document Building an Inclusive Society, Dublin, Stationery Office.

Department of the Environment (1995), *Social Housing — The Way Ahead*, Dublin.

Department of the Environment (various), *Housing Statistics Bulletin*, Dublin, Stationery Office.

Department of the Environment and Local Government (2000), *Action on Housing*, Dublin.

Department of the Environment and Local Government (2000), *Report of the Commission on The Private Rented Residential Sector*, Dublin, Stationery Office.

Duffy, D., J. Fitzgerald, J. Kearney, J. Hore and C. MacCoille (2001), *Medium–Term Review: 2001–2007*, Dublin, ESRI.

Education (Welfare) Act, 2000.

Education Act, 1998.

European Commission (2000) *Public finances in EMU — 2000 Report of the Directorate General for Economic and Financial Affairs*, Luxembourg.

Eurostat (2001), *Eurostat yearbook 2001*, Luxembourg.

Eurostat (1999), 'Social benefits and their redistributive effect in the EU', in *Statistics in Focus, Theme 3 – 13/1999*, Luxembourg.

Eurostat (2001), *Expenditure on Social Protection*, Luxembourg.

Fahey, Tony (1998), *Housing and Social Cohesion: Making Local Authority Housing Effective*, John Blackwell Memorial Lecture, Housing Institute of Ireland.

Fingleton, W.A. (December 1995), 'Structural Change in Dairying in Ireland and the EU: Actual and Projected', Paper presented at Conference on Dairy and Beef Industries, Dublin, Teagasc.

Fischler, F. (10 November 1997), 'LEADER: Ideas and Initiatives for Development', Opening Address to the LEADER Symposium, Brussels.

Focus Ireland (2001), *Housing Initiative*, Dublin.

Focus Ireland (2002), *Housing waiting list Survey 2001,* Dublin.

Galbraith, J.K. (1992), *The Culture of Contentment*, Sinclair-Stevenson.

Gray, A.W. (1997), *International Perspectives on the Irish Economy*, Dublin, Indecon.

Healy, S. and B. Reynolds (1998), 'Progress, Paradigms and Policy', in Healy, S. and B. Reynolds (eds.)' *Social Policy in Ireland: Principles, Practice and Problems*, Dublin, Oak Tree Press.

Healy, S. and B. Reynolds (eds.) (1998), *Social Policy in Ireland: Principles Practice and Problems*, Dublin, Oak Tree Press.

Healy, S. and B. Reynolds (1993), 'Work, Jobs and Income: Towards a New Paradigm', in B. Reynolds and S. Healy (eds.), *New Frontiers for Full Citizenship*, Dublin, CMRS.

Healy, S. and B. Reynolds (1999), 'Towards a New Vision of Social Partnership: Values, Content, Process and Structure' in Healy, S. and B. Reynolds (eds.), *Social Partnership in a New Century,* Dublin, CORI.

Heater, D. (1990), *Citizenship,* London, Longman.

Interaction Council (1996), *In Search of Global Ethical Standards*, Vancouver, Interaction Council.

Kearney, C. (ed.) (1999), *Budget Perspective*, Dublin, ESRI.

Layte, R., B. Maitre, B. Nolan, W. Watson, C.T. Whelan, J. Williams, and B. Casey (2001), *Monitoring Poverty Trends and Exploring Poverty Dynamics in Ireland*, Dublin, ESRI.

Lister, R. (1998), Citizenship*: Feminist Perspectives*, London, Macmillan.

McCashin, A. (2000*), The Private Rented Sector in the 21st Century — Policy Choices*. Dublin, Threshold and St Pancras Housing Association.

McCoy, D. (various), *Quarterly Economic Commentary*, Dublin, ESRI.

McCoy, S, A. Doyle and J. Williams (1999), *1998 Annual School Leavers' Survey of 1996/97 Leavers,* Dublin, ESRI/Department of Education and Science/Department of Enterprise, Trade and Employment.

Mead, L. (1986), *Beyond Entitlement: The Social Obligation of Citizenship,* New York, The Free Press.

Mkandawire, T. and V. Rodriguez (2000), *Globalization and Social Development after Copenhagen: Premises, Promises and Policies,* Geneva 2000 Occasional Paper 10, Geneva, UNRISD.

National Action Plan against Poverty and Social Exclusion (2001), Dublin, Stationery Office.

National Anti-Poverty Strategy (1997), *Sharing in Progress*, Dublin, Stationery Office.

National Economic and Social Council (2000), *Opportunities, Challenges and Capacities for Choice,* Dublin, NESC.

National Economic and Social Council (2001), *Review of the Poverty Proofing Process,* Dublin, NESC.

National Economic and Social Council (1988), *Redistribution Through State Social Expenditure in the Republic of Ireland: 1973–80,* Dublin, NESC.

National Economic and Social Council (1996), *Strategy into the 21st Century,* Dublin, NESC.

National Economic and Social Forum (1996), *Equality Proofing Issues*, Dublin.

National Economic and Social Forum (1997), *A Framework for Partnership — Enriching Strategic Consensus through Participation,* Dublin.

National Economic and Social Forum (1997). *Early School Leaving and Youth Unemployment.* Forum Report No. 11. Dublin: National Economic and Social Forum.

Nolan, B. (2000), *Child Poverty in Ireland,* Dublin, Combat Poverty Agency.

References

Nolan, B. and T. Callan (1994), *Poverty and Policy in Ireland*, Dublin, Gill and Macmillan.

Novak, MD., J. Cogan, B. Bernstein et al. (1987), *A Community of Self-Reliance: The New Consensus on Family and Welfare,* Milwaukee, American Institute for Public Policy Research.

O'Hara, P. and P. Commins (1998), 'Rural Development: Towards the New Century', in S. Healy and B. Reynolds (1998), *Social Policy in Ireland: Principles, Practice and Problems*, Dublin, Oak Tree Press, pp. 261–283.

OECD (2001), *Economic Outlook.*

OECD (2001), *International Adult Literacy Survey.*

Oldfield, A. (1990), *Citizenship and Community: Civic Republicanism and the Modern World,* London, Routledge.

Oliver, D. and D. Heater (1994), *The Foundations of Citizenship*, Hemel Hempstead, Harvester Wheatsheaf.

Partnership 2000 (1998), *Report of Social Economy Working Group,* Final Report submitted to government.

Partnership 2000 for Inclusion, Employment and Competitiveness, (1996), Dublin, Stationery Office.

Powell, F. and D.K.L. Guerin (1997), *Civil Society and Social Policy,* Dublin, Farmar.

Programme for Prosperity and Fairness (2000), Dublin, Stationery Office.

Programme for Prosperity and Fairness (2001), *Final Report of the Social Welfare Benchmarking and Indexation Group*, Dublin.

Report of the Expert Working Group on the Integration of the Tax and Social Welfare Systems (1996), Dublin, Stationery Office.

Reynolds, B. and S. Healy (eds.) (1993), *New Frontiers for Full Citizenship*, Dublin, CMRS.

Reynolds, B. and S. Healy (eds.)(1996), *Progress, Values and Public Policy*, Dublin, CORI.

Robertson, J. (1994), *Benefits and Taxes: A Radical Strategy,* London, The New Economics Foundation.

Robertson, J. (1997), *The New Economics of Sustainable Development,* Report to the European Commission, Brussels.

Smyth, E. (1999), 'Educational Inequalities Among School Leavers in Ireland 1979–1994', in *The Economic and Social Review,* Vol. 30, No. 3, July 1999, pp. 267–84.

Steering Group on the Funding of Second Level Schools (June 1999). *Funding of Second Level Schools: Report of the Steering Group,* Dublin, Government Publications.

Task Force on the Travelling Community (July 1995), Final Report, Dublin, Stationery Office.

Threshold (2001), *Budget 2002: a real response to crises in housing?,* Dublin, Threshold.

Towards an Independent Future (1996), Report of the Review Group on Health and Personal Social Services for People with Physical and Sensory Disabilities, Dublin, Stationery Office.

UNAIDS (2001), *AIDS epidemic update December 2001,* UNAIDS/WHO, Switzerland.

United Nations Development Program (2001), *Human Development Report — 2001,* New York, United Nations Publications.

Vincentian Partnership for Social Justice (2001), *One Long Struggle, a study of low income families,* Dublin.

Waltzer, M. (1983), *Spheres of Justice. A Defence of Pluralism and Equality,* Oxford, Oxford University Press.

Whelan, C. and D. Hannan (1999), 'Class Inequalities in Educational Attainment', in *The Economic and Social Review,* Vol. 30, No. 3, July 1999, pp. 285–307.

Williams J. and M. O'Connor (1999), *Counted In: The Report of the 1999 Assessment of Homelessness in Dublin, Kildare and Wicklow,* Dublin, ESRI.

Wogaman, J.P. (1986), *Economics and Ethics: A Christian Enquiry,* London, SCM Press.